WOOD CARVING
23 Traditional Decorative Projects

WOOD CARVING

23 Traditional Decorative Projects

Alan & Gill Bridgewater

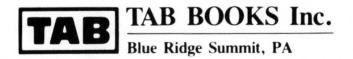

TAB BOOKS Inc.

Blue Ridge Summit, PA

FIRST EDITION
FIRST PRINTING

Copyright © 1988 by TAB BOOKS Inc.
Printed in the United States of America

Library of Congress Cataloging in Publication Data
Bridgewater, Alan.
Wood carving.

Bibliography: p.
Includes index.
1. Wood-carving.   I. Bridgewater, Gill.   II. Title.
TT199.7.B76 1988   736′.4   88-2160
ISBN 0-8306-0979-2
ISBN 0-8306-2979-3 (pbk.)

Questions regarding the content of this book
should be addressed to:

Reader Inquiry Branch
TAB BOOKS Inc.
Blue Ridge Summit, PA 17294-0214

TAB BOOKS Inc. offers software for sale.
For information and a catalog, please contact TAB Software Department,
Blue Ridge Summit, PA 17294-0850.

Edited by Suzanne L. Cheatle
Designed by Jaclyn B. Saunders

Contents

Introduction   *xi*

Workshop Data   *1*

Project 1   *18*

MAKING A ROOSTER
WEATHER VANE SCULPTURE
IN THE AMERICAN COLONIAL TRADITION

Project 2   *27*

CARVING AND PAINTING A HOUSE SIGNBOARD
IN THE OLD ENGLISH TRADITION

Project 3   *37*

WHITTLING A LOVE SPOON
IN THE WELSH TRADITION

Project 4   *47*

CARVING A TULIP PANEL IN THE
ENGLISH JACOBEAN FLAT-RELIEF TRADITION

Project 5   *57*

MAKING A WHIRLIGIG IN THE
ENGLISH AND AMERICAN TRADITION

Project 6   *67*

MAKING A STENCILED AND PAINTED CHECKER
BOARD IN THE AMERICAN FOLK TRADITION

77 Project 7

CARVING A BISCUIT MOLD IN THE
PENNSYLVANIA DUTCH SPRINGERLE
BOARD TRADITION

86 Project 8

CARVING AND PAINTING
A CIGAR-STORE INDIAN IN THE
AMERICAN "VIRGINIAN" TRADITION

96 Project 9

PAINTING A HOPE CHEST IN THE
18TH CENTURY TRADITION

106 Project 10

CARVING AND PAINTING A WILD FOWL DECOY
IN THE AMERICAN GUNNER TRADITION

117 Project 11

WORKING A CHIP-CARVED SERVING BOARD
IN THE MEDIEVAL ENGLISH TRADITION

127 Project 12

TURNING AND CARVING A PASTRY ROLLER
IN THE ENGLISH TREEN TRADITION

137 Project 13

MAKING A NURSERY COMFORT BOARD
IN THE ENGLISH AND AMERICAN TRADITION

Project 14 147

MAKING AN OVAL STEAM-BENT CARRIER IN THE AMERICAN SHAKER TRADITION

Project 15 157

MAKING A HANGING SHELF IN THE ENGLISH AND AMERICAN COUNTRY KITCHEN TRADITION

Project 16 167

WHITTLING AND PAINTING A MR. PUNCH PUPPET HEAD IN THE ENGLISH TRADITION

Project 17 177

DECORATING FURNITURE IN THE AMERICAN STENCIL TRADITION

Project 18 187

MAKING AND DECORATING A SALT BOX IN THE AMERICAN FRACTUR TRADITION

Project 19 198

MAKING AND PAINTING ROUNDELS IN THE ENGLISH ELIZABETHAN TRADITION

Project 20 208

MAKING A FRETWORK AND CHIP-CARVED DISTAFF IN THE ENGLISH AND AMERICAN FOLK TRADITION

219 Project 21

MAKING A BOWL IN THE ENGLISH
POLE LATHE GREENWOOD TRADITION

228 Project 22

MAKING A CRADLE IN
THE AMERICAN PILGRIM TRADITION

237 Project 23

MAKING AND CARVING A
PLANK-BACK SPINNING STOOL
IN THE COUNTRY-COTTAGE TRADITION

249 Further Reading

251 Index

Wood is both beautiful and easy to work. For centuries making decorative woodwork has been exciting and stimulating, if necessary, homemaking activity. The term *decorative folk woodwork* describes all the functional and beautifully decorative items that have always been made by ordinary uncultured folk. Painted chests, carved chairs, boxes, shelves, bowls, platters, and cradles are all part and parcel of what has come to be known as the decorative folk woodwork tradition.

Introduction

What is decorative folk woodwork? In the simplest possible terms, it is the craft woodwork of the people, the decorative woodwork of your folks and mine. Of course, I realize that this definition is a bit hazy, but how better can we describe, and put a name to, all the necessary and beautifully decorative items of woodwork that have always been made by ordinary uncultured folk? So there you have it, if it is made of wood, if it is unpretentious and of a primitive, naive country character, then it is a piece of decorative folk woodwork.

Of course, there is more to it than that. Certainly we can all understand how and why our grandparents and great-grandparents made domestic functional items like pastry rollers, bowls, and cradles, but how were these selfsame so-called *ordinary folk* also able to decorate their woodwork with wonderful swirling chip-carved designs, rhythmic incised patterns, and dynamic painted motifs? Well, in times past, woodworking traditions and skills were passed on by word of mouth from father to son and mother to daughter. So, for example, when the nine-teenth century American backwoods settler made a piece of woodwork for the home, he was not only making a salt box, a spoon rack, or whatever, he was patterning and designing in a way that related to all the customs and traditions of his Old-World forefathers.

Away with definitions, questions, and generalizations. It is enough to know that decorative folk woodwork looks back to a time when unsophisticated people carved wood and made all manner of wonderfully decorative folk-art items.

This book is about personal, pleasuresome hand-on-tool involvement: run-ning your hands over a rough-sawn wood, letting your fingertips play over a carving or a whittling, looking at a box or love spoon that you have made. These are all wonderful, creative, physical, and spiritual pioneer experiences that should not be missed. By working through the projects in this book, you will not only enrich your home, you will once again relive those mind-out-of-time, folk-remembered craft experiences that are part of your past and mine. Soon you will look to those warm, long-grass days of long ago when you were first given a sharp knife and let loose in the woods. The marvelous feeling of whittling and carving soft, sweet-smelling hedgerow sticks, the thrill of seeing the bark roll back, the scent of the warm sap, and the satisfaction of patterning the smooth, white, moist wood.

If you have a yearning to carve your own house sign, to make a whirligig, to whittle a love spoon, to fashion a comfort board, to paint a hope chest, or to make any number of other traditional folk-inspired woodwork projects, then this book is for you. Don't be inhibited or even give a thought to power drills, overcomplicated textbook joints, and all those other horrors of modern woodworking because this book is about the empirical close feel of tool and materials. Enjoy looking at our designs and motifs, study our working drawings, follow our hints and tips, and then either make our projects as is, or modify and adjust them to suit your own design and material inclinations.

Follow through the traditional designs, patterns, and motifs and walk in the footsteps of your pioneer and country rustic forefathers. What could be more stimulating than to take a slab of found wood, a few simple tools, some brushes, and bright primary colors, and make your own unique piece of decorative folk woodwork?

Workshop Data

ACRYLIC PAINT A type of water-based paint belonging to the acrylic resin family. These paints dry in a few hours, and they are very easy to use. Once dry, acrylics can be varnished or glazed to give a high-gloss finish. A word of caution: because acrylics do dry so very fast, either let your brushes stand in water or, better still, wash them under running water as soon as possible.

ADZE An axelike cutting tool that has a curved blade set at right angles to a wooden handle or shaft. In use, an adze is swung in an arch to remove little scoops of wood.

APPLE WOOD A beautiful dense-grained hardwood that carves well and takes a good polish.

ASH A long-grained, difficult-to-work hardwood, not suitable for beginners.

AXE A tool for wood preparation and roughing-out. Such tools come in all shapes, sizes, and patterns.

BEECH A pleasant hardwood, relatively easy to work, reddish brown in color, with a straight, close grain.

BEESWAX A yellowish or dark brown wax secreted by honeybees for constructing honeycombs. In solid or paste form it is used for polishing.

BENT For gouges, referring to curved types that have the same cutting section as straight chisels and gouges. The names of such tools usually describe their shape and/or their use, for example a *bowl back-bent* and a *relief ground dog-leg*.

BLEMISH   A loose knot, rust, grease stain, split, or such in wood. Depending on the project, unusual grain colors and strange knot formations might or might not be considered blemishes.

BOW SAW   A saw having an H-shaped frame and a thin, flexible blade. It is used for cutting and shaping thin plank wood.

BOXWOOD   A dense-grained hardwood, with a beautiful butter color, perfect for special carvings.

BRIDGE   1) A slender piece of supporting wood that is left in place when working a delicate pierced carving. 2) A piece of wood that is subsequently cut away. 3) A slender area of stencil card between two cut-away "windows."

BRUSHES   For decorative woodworking, we use large, soft, broad, and fine-pointed bristles set in a handle. They improve with use, so buy the best and keep them clean.

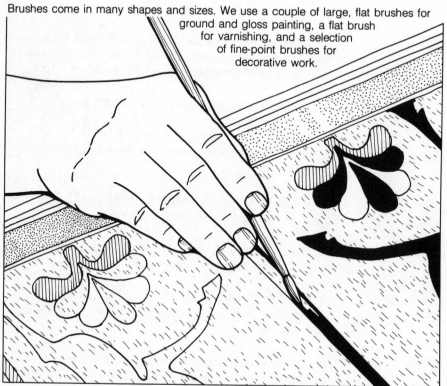

Brushes come in many shapes and sizes. We use a couple of large, flat brushes for ground and gloss painting, a flat brush for varnishing, and a selection of fine-point brushes for decorative work.

BURNISHING	The act of taking a piece of wood to a high-shine finish. It is best achieved using oil, beeswax, a cloth, and a lot of effort.
CALIPERS	A two-legged distance and measurement transference tool. It can be used for inside and outside turned work.
CHECK	A split or crack in a piece of wood. If possible reject such timber.
CHERRY	A close-grained hardwood, red-brown in color, that carves well.
CHESTNUT	A beautiful compact brown hardwood that carves well.
CHIP CARVING	A traditional folk technique of decorating the surfaces of wooden objects by chipping out little triangular pockets. By repeatedly cutting organized patterns of pockets, it is possible to achieve the most startling carved patterns and designs. Chip carving is simple and easy to do; it is in fact the perfect carving technique for beginners.

Chip carving is a technique of decorating a smooth surface by repeatedly chipping out little triangular pockets of wood. It is best to use a small short-bladed, skew-edged knife.

CHIP-CARVING KNIFE	A short-bladed skew-edged knife used for working chip-carved designs.
CHISEL	A flat-bladed hand tool. In use it is held in one hand and pushed or struck.
CLAMP (Brit: CRAMP)	A screw device used for holding two pieces of wood together or for securing wood to the bench while it is being worked. Types include C-clamps (Brit: G-clamps), sash cramps, strap clamps, holdfasts, and so on.
COMPASS	A two-legged instrument used for drawing circles and arcs.

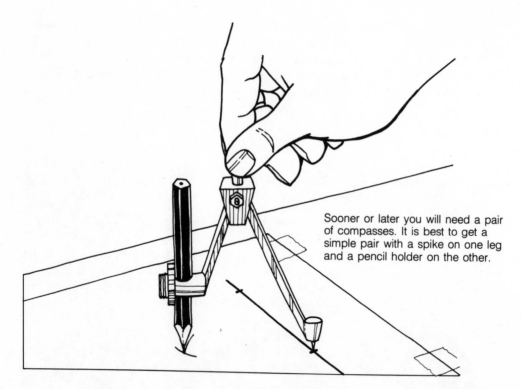

Sooner or later you will need a pair of compasses. It is best to get a simple pair with a spike on one leg and a pencil holder on the other.

| CLOSE-GRAINED | Referring to wood that looks to have evenly set annual rings. Such wood carves well. |
| COPING SAW | A fine-bladed saw used for fretting out thin section wood, the blade is held in a C-shaped metal frame. Because the blade can be quickly removed and refitted, this type of saw is ideal for cutting holes and for working awkward corners and angles (see illustration on page 5). |

A coping saw has a fine, flexible blade tensioned in a steel **C** frame. The swivel handle allows for instant blade removal and cutting in any direction. It is the perfect tool for working holes and complex profiles in thin-sectioned wood.

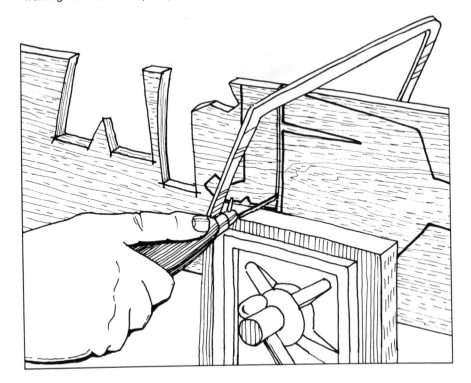

DECAY
Discoloration, rot, or sponginess on a piece of timber. Do not use such wood for woodworking.

DRAWKNIFE
A two-handed tool used for cutting free shapes. In use it is held in both hands and drawn toward the user.

DESIGNING
By way of museum research, the process of sketching, making working drawings, and building models and prototypes to design a unique form or structure (see illustrations on page 6).

DRILL
A hole-making device. Types include brace and bit drills, small drills, bench drills, power drills, and so on. We advocate using a small, silent running, hand-operated drill for decorative woodworking.

ELEVATIONS
In drawing, the various views of an object as seen from the front, side, and top.

Pencils and a plastic set square need
to be used at the designing stage.

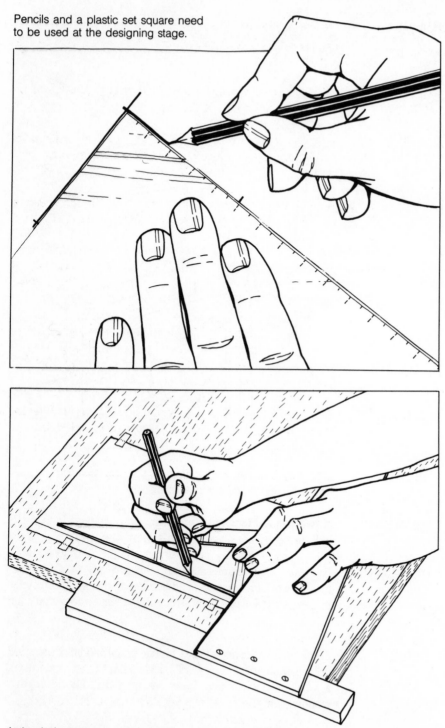

At the design stage, you will need a drawing board, a set square, and a **T** square. Organize
your working area so that one corner can be set aside for drawing and painting.

FINISH   To burnish, rub down with sandpapers, wipe with wax, paint, or otherwise enhance the textural and visual appearance of a piece of wood.

FIRST CUTS   When the woodworking tools are being used for the first time; the stage that follows designing.

FOUND WOOD   Wood salvaged from forestry works, odds and ends from building sites, branches found on country walks, old ship timbers found when beachcombing, etc.

FILLER   A substance used to fill cracks and cavities in the wood. It is best to use a two-part resin filler of the type used to patch car bodies.

FRETSAW   Akin to a coping saw, a saw with a thin flexible blade set in a large G frame. It is the perfect tool for cutting "windows" and complex profiles in thin plywood and planks.

GLUES   An adhesive product. There are hundreds of products to choose from—rubber glues in tubes, glues in cans, hot glue guns, two-tube resins etc. In the context of this book we favor easy-to-use polyvinyl acetate glue. See PVA.

GOUGE   A curve-sectioned chisel. There are hundreds of different types. In use a gouge is held in one hand and pushed or struck.

GREENWOOD   Wood that contains sap. Also called *unseasoned*, or *wet*, wood.

GRID   Guide and scale lines that are drawn onto plans; lines that are drawn onto the working face of the wood to be carved. Our working drawing grid squares can be read-off as units of measurement.

GROUNDING   *See* wasting.

HARDWOOD   Botanically, a wood from a deciduous tree. Not all such woods are actually hard in texture. For example, balsa is termed a hardwood.

HOLLY   A close-grained, creamy white, hardwood. It is a beautiful wood to carve and turn.

INCISED CARVING   The process of drawing designs out on wood and then cutting the lines in with either a knife or a V-section tool. With incised work, there is no modeling; the V-section cuts are in themselves the total design.

Many of the projects in this book might be described as complicated. For example, the biscuit mold design needs to be cut in with incised lines and then overworked with scoop tools. If you want to simplify the project, however, then there's no reason why you shouldn't redesign the motifs and have them worked entirely in incised line.

INSPIRATIONAL MATERIAL   Magazine clips, museum exhibits, craft-center handouts, books, films, etc., used to inspire you in a project.

KEYHOLE SAW   A thin-bladed knife-like saw used for cutting out slots and holes. Also called a *pad saw*.

KNIFE   A cutting tool. In the context of this book, a good knife might be an expensive special or just an old kitchen knife. If it fits the purpose, then it's suitable.

KNOTS   The portion of a tree branch that appears in the face or edge of a finished piece of lumber. Types include: dead, hollow, live, and loose. Depending on your viewpoint, such features might or might not be desirable. Knots tend to be difficult to work.

LATHE   A machine for shaping or turning wood. In turning, the workpiece is spun against a hand-held cutting tool.

The pole lathe is a beautiful piece of low-tech equipment, simple to make and easy to use. If you intend to make chairs and bowls using greenwood, then this is the machine for you. (See Project 21.)

LIME	A close-grained, knot-free wood that comes in large sizes. It can be more or less carved and worked in any direction, and is a good wood for beginners.
LOWERING	Wasting, grounding, or cutting away background wood.
MAHOGANY	A red-brown hardwood, straight grained and easy to work. Various types include: Cuban, American, African, etc.
MALLET	A hammer or club used for gouge and chisel striking. The best ones are made of beech.
MARKING OUT	The transferring of the lines of the design to one or other of the working faces of the wood.
MAQUETTE	A working model that is made prior to using the best wood. This model might be made from card, modeling paste, clay, wax, soap, or even an inexpensive wood.
OAK	A hardwood. From tree to tree, oak can be easy to carve, difficult to carve, or tool-breaking; attractive, or plain. This being so, choose your wood with care.
OFF-CUTS	Small pieces of wood left over at the end of a project; scraps of wood that can be purchased from timber suppliers.
PAINTING	The process of covering a surface with a colored, opaque finish. When you come to painting start by making sure that the project is clean and free from dust, then set it out in a dust-free environment. When your work area is organized and all your tools and materials are at hand, prepare the paint as described by the manufacturer. The order of work will, of course, depend on what sort of paints you are using and the type of effect you desire. If, however, you do have doubts as to how to use a certain paint, then take a piece of scrap wood through all the painting stages (see illustration at top of page 10.)
PEAR	A pinkish-brown hardwood. It comes in relatively small sizes and is a beautiful wood to carve.
PENCIL	A writing implement, usually containing graphite as the marking substance. Use a soft **2B** for designing and tracing, and a hard **H** for pencil-press transferring.

When you come to painting, it is best to work outside the woodworking area. Many traditional folk designs were achieved by multiple techniques. For example, with this checkerboard, the checker grid and the main bird and flower forms are stenciled, and the little decorative details are brush-worked.

PENCIL-PRESS TRANSFERRING	The process of taking a tracing from a master design, reversing or penciling in the back of the tracing, and pressing through with a pencil so as to transfer the traced lines through to the working surface of the wood.
PIERCING	The act of cutting a hole in a piece of wood, or making an undercut that goes under some part of the project.
PULLING TOGETHER	The act of assembling the various components, or rethinking or reworking the designs.

PVA GLUE	A woodworking glue/adhesive that belongs to the polyvinyl acetate family. Such glues are easy to prepare, easy to use, water based, and altogether pleasant and suitable for the projects in this book.
PINE	A white/yellow softwood. There are many varieties, all with different qualities, so choose your wood with care.
PLUM	A brown hardwood that takes a good finish.
PROFILES	In the context of this book, any cutout, flat shape, side view, cross section, or silhouette.
PROTOTYPE	A working model or maquette made prior to making the project. If you aren't quite sure as to form, size, shape or suitability, it is best to make a prototype.
QUICK FINISH	A finish that is swift, direct, and uncomplicated; an unfussed finish.
RELIEF CARVING	A logical extension of incised carving. Once designs have been drawn out and cut in, the carver sets in and wastes or grounds the carving. With gouges and other scoop tools, the carver lowers all the wood that is considered to be outside the design. Once the waste has been cut away, he models and carves the relief areas so that they have depth, shape, and form.
RIFFLERS	A small double-ended file used for working awkward corners and crannies.
ROUGHING-OUT	The act of cutting away unwanted wood.
RUBBING DOWN	The process of using a graded pack of sandpapers/glasspapers/grits to rub the surface of the wood until it is smooth to the touch. Rubbing down is messy and so best done outdoors.
SAPWOOD	Wet wood just under the bark. Use sapwood with caution.
SEASONED WOOD	Wood that has a low moisture content. Wood is variously described as green, wet, half-seasoned, and seasoned.
SETTING IN	The act of transferring the pencil-drawn design to the working face of the wood and then to cutting-in the design with an edged tool. Sometimes taken to mean the first cuts.

SETTING OUT	The act of transferring the traced designs through to the working face of the wood.
SHAKE	A split, cavity, or separation that occurs throughout log lengths. Such features should be viewed with suspicion.
SHORT GRAIN	Areas of the wood where the structure of the grain is such that the wood is fragile and liable to split.
SKETCHBOOK	A bound book containing plain paper, in which to keep all museum studies. Don't do your sketches on scraps of paper.
SLIPSTONE	A small, shaped stone used to keep a good cutting edge on gouges and chisels.
SOFTWOOD	Botanically, a wood from a coniferous tree.
STENCIL CARD	A stiff waxed, oiled, or varnished card used for making templates and stencils.
STENCILING	The art and craft of applying a painted design, motif, or pattern by cutting "windows" in thin card, plastic, or metal, and then brushing paint through the holes onto the surface to be decorated (see illustration on page 14).
STOP CUTS	A cut that stops short and contains subsequent cuts.
SURFORM	A trademark for a planelike rasp used for working and shaping free forms.
SYCAMORE	A light-colored hardwood. It is a good wood for carving and turning.
TOOLED FINISH	A texture or finish that relates to the marks left by the tools. Each tool leaves its own characteristic mark (see pages 16 and 17).
TRACING PAPER	A strong transparent paper used at the design stage. It is best to use a good-quality grade. In use, a tracing is taken from the master drawing, the tracing is lined in on the reverse side, and finally a hard pencil is used to press transfer the traced lines through to the working face of the wood.
TRENCHING	The act of cutting in and establishing the pencil-drawn lines with a V-section tool. Also called V-cutting.

Stenciling is a beautifully easy method of achieving vigorous painted designs and motifs. Holes are cut in the stencil plate and paint is brushed through the holes onto the surface that is to be decorated. By overlapping the design and only stippling the edge of the motif, you can create designs in the Hitchcock tradition. (See Project 17.)

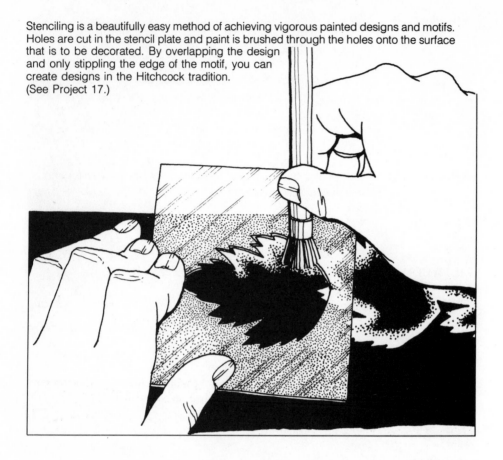

V-SECTION TOOL	Any gouge that cuts a V-section trench.
VISE	A bench-mounted screw clamp, used for securing wood while it is being worked. Also called *carver's chops*.
WASTE GROUND	Wood that occurs behind or around a motif; background wood; wood that needs to be cut away and/or lowered.
WHITTLING	From the Anglo-Saxon word *thwitan*, meaning to cut and pare wood with a small knife. In the modern sense, the word has come to describe the technique of making small spontaneous carved items like paper knives, small figures, chains, and animals.
WOODWORKING TOOL	In the context of this book, any basic, simple-to-use, traditional, hand-held tool that might be used to work wood.

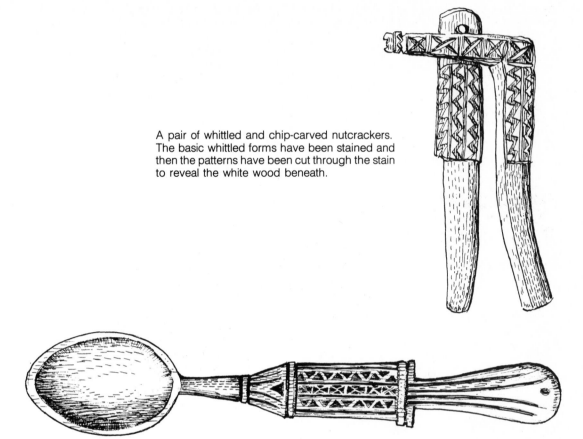

A pair of whittled and chip-carved nutcrackers. The basic whittled forms have been stained and then the patterns have been cut through the stain to reveal the white wood beneath.

A whittled and chip-carved love spoon.

WORKBENCH	A stable, strong work surface. In the context of this book, a wood carver's trestle, the kitchen table, or a carpenter's bench with a vise.
WORKING DRAWINGS	Carefully considered drawings; scaled and measured drawings that show all views.
WORKING FACE	The best side of the wood; the side that shows the important face.
WORKOUTS	Drawings, experimental work, models, or maquettes.
YEW	A fine, yellow, hardwood. It cuts cleanly and takes a good polish.

WOODWORKING TOOLS:

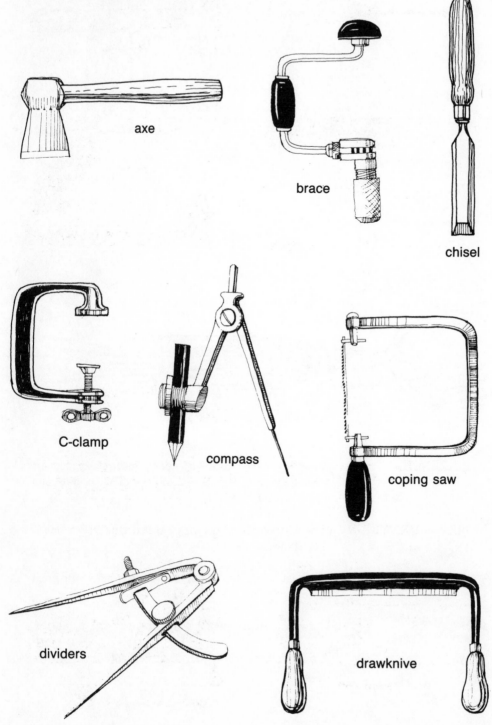

axe

brace

chisel

C-clamp

compass

coping saw

dividers

drawknive

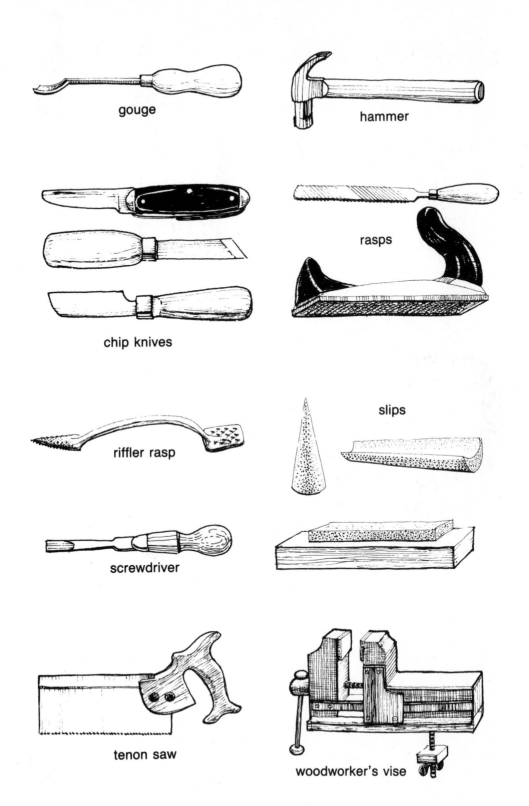

gouge

hammer

chip knives

rasps

riffler rasp

slips

screwdriver

tenon saw

woodworker's vise

PROJECT 1

MAKING A
Rooster Weather Vane Sculpture
IN THE
American Colonial Tradition

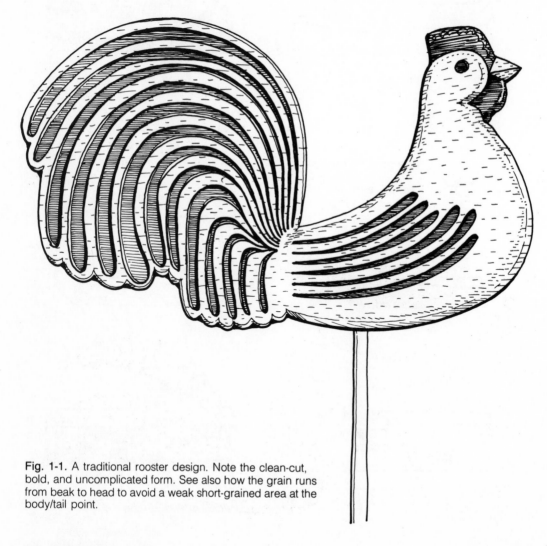

Fig. 1-1. A traditional rooster design. Note the clean-cut, bold, and uncomplicated form. See also how the grain runs from beak to head to avoid a weak short-grained area at the body/tail point.

Fig. 1-2. Traditional inspirational designs

A horse and foal

A dragon/serpent

An angel

A goose

In the pretechnological world of the early American, in villages and small towns where every other man was either a sailor or a farmer, it was vital to "keep one's weather eye open." In fact, it is no exaggeration to say that for those pioneers, their very life and fortune depended upon being able to predict the next spell of good or bad weather. This being so, it is hardly surprising that primitive paintings from the Colonial period show rooftops bristling with that most reliable of meteorological instruments: the weather vane (FIG 1-1).

Cut from sawn plank or split slab wood, swiftly worked with a knife and gouge, and then painted with bold, direct earth colors, these weather vanes, or *wind flags*, were of course more than just weather-reporting machines. They were trade signs, shop signs, good-luck symbols, and so on. The early Colonial carvers favored simple, dramatic design themes—horses, Indians, roosters, serpents, and fish—all strong, bold, meaningful, easily worked motifs that could be clearly seen at a distance when silhouetted against the sky (FIG. 1-2).

Materials

A 1-inch-thick, 14-x-24-inch plank of straight-grained, knot-free, lightweight wood (you could try lime or pine)
A couple of tins of acrylic paint, colors to suit

Tools

A sketchbook
A large sheet of work-out paper
A large sheet of tracing paper
Brushes
A bow saw or a large coping saw
A couple of clasp knives
A couple of gouges (you might use a straight, a spoon bit, and a curved gouge)
Other workshop items, like sandpaper and old rags

DESIGN AND TECHNIQUE

Look at your inspirational illustrations and the working drawings (FIG. 1-3), and see how early weather vanes have characteristically bold profiles, meaning the forms are clean-cut and uncomplicated. Note also how the designs relate directly to the run of the grain and the use of a few basic traditional hand tools. For example, the rooster, the angel, and the goose all have the grain running horizontally so that there is a minimum of weak short grain. They could all be worked with the bow saw, the gouge, and the knife.

Now stop awhile and consider just how you want your weather vane to be. For example, do you want to make a full-size working machine, or are you (as in this project) going to use sawn plank wood and carve and paint a weather

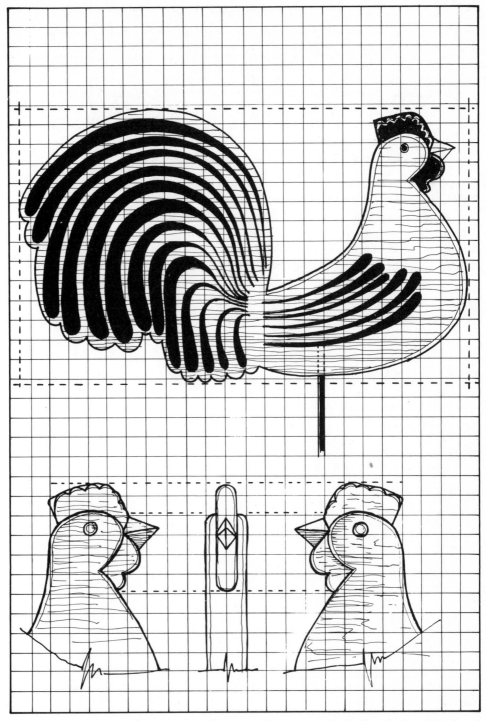

Fig. 1-3. Working drawings—the scale is about 1 grid square to 1 inch. Note the head detail and see how at the beak and comb the wood has been cut away and reduced.

vane sculpture in the Colonial folk-art tradition? If you can, visit a folk-art museum, and search out wood-carved weather vanes of the Colonial and Early American period. Look at how they fit the slab wood, note the shallow swift carving, and see how they are painted with striking combinations of a few basic colors.

After you have considered all these points, make a series of design sketches. Finally, when you have achieved what you consider to be a good working design, make a full-size master drawing and a tracing.

Setting Out the Wood and First Cuts

First check your wood over and make sure that it's free from end splits, dead knots, and bad grain twists. This done, set the wood out on the workbench and pencil-press transfer the traced lines of the design through to the working face of the wood (FIG. 1-4). Now take a soft pencil, thicken up the profile lines and cross hatch, and clearly label all the areas of waste. At this stage, don't worry too much about the details; just establish the main profile outline.

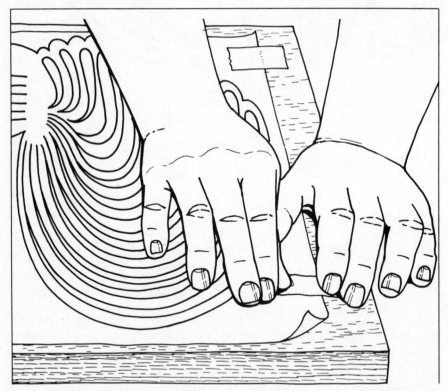

Fig. 1-4. Trace the design, line-in the back of the tracing, secure the tracing with a few tabs of masking tape, and then pencil-press transfer the traced lines through to the working face of the wood.

After you have transferred the design, secure the wood in the vise or clamp it flat down on the bench, and then use the bow saw to fret out the basic rooster form (FIG. 1-5). Bearing in mind that you will need to keep turning the blade in its frame, and to keep repositioning the wood in the vise, maneuver the saw around the form. Try not to wrench or force the blade at the sharp angles. If need be, make new cuts in from the edge of the plank and remove the waste one wedge at a time. Cut on the waste side of the drawn lines and, as you are working, hold the saw so that the blade is at right angles to the working face of the wood.

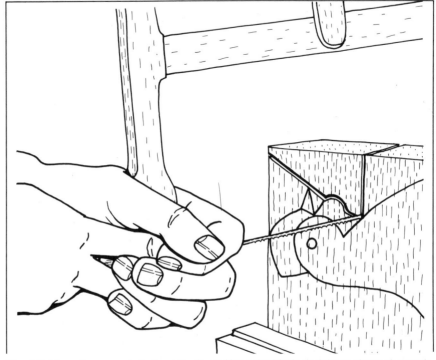

Fig. 1-5. Use a bow saw to fret out the form. Keep the blade at right angles to the working face of the wood, and be careful that you don't twist and break the blade.

Knife-Working the Head

When you have cleared away the waste, take one of your chosen knives and run it around the sawn edge, removing all the sharp corners. Have a look at the working drawings and note how the rooster's comb and beak details have been lowered and modeled.

Now take the knife and make V-cuts around the head. Hold the knife as if you are going to peel an apple and then make sliding paring cuts into the initial V-section stop cuts. Lower the wood either side of the comb until the original 1-inch thickness is down to about ½ inch (FIG. 1-6).

Continue until you have established the comb and the beak. Don't fuss around trying for realism; just go for the overall form.

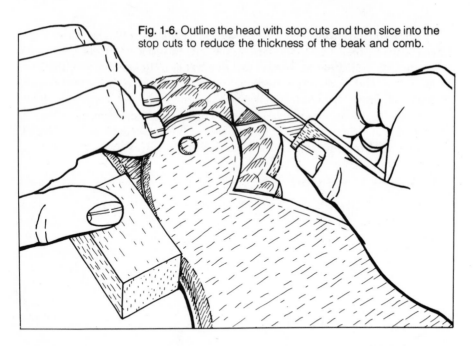

Fig. 1-6. Outline the head with stop cuts and then slice into the stop cuts to reduce the thickness of the beak and comb.

Carving the Feathers

Reestablish the transferred pencil lines, take note of the beautiful smooth-lined sweep of the tail, then take the knife and set-in the individual simplified feather forms (FIG. 1-7). Cut-in V-section trenches to a depth of about ⅛ inch.

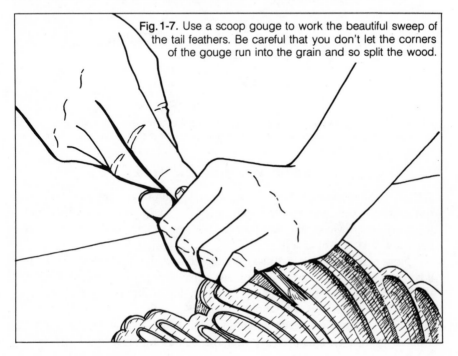

Fig. 1-7. Use a scoop gouge to work the beautiful sweep of the tail feathers. Be careful that you don't let the corners of the gouge run into the grain and so split the wood.

This done, take one of your chosen gouges, note the direction of the grain, then slide the tool around the individual feathers and remove crisp curls of wood. Don't try to work each of the feathers in a single great wood-digging stroke, but rather go at it little by little, all the while noting the direction of the grain in relation to the angle of cut. Cut either across or at an angle to the grain.

Work all the feathers in this way, establishing the outline with V-cuts, lowering the waste with a curved gouge, reestablishing the knife cut, gouging deeper, and so on until you have achieved the beautiful and characteristic sweep of pattern.

PAINTING AND FINISHING

When you have worked the head with a knife and carved the various feathers with a gouge, then go over the whole carving with a knife and a gouge and bring the wood to order. Cut in the eyes, cut in the delicate comb scalloping, trim away rough edges and burrs, and generally make the carving good.

Next, have a look at your various design sketches and museum notes, and make decisions as to the base or ground color, and the feather and comb details. Note that this project uses a traditional color scheme; that is to say, the ground and beak are painted with yellow ochre to simulate gilt, and the comb and feathers are painted brilliant red.

When you have chosen your colors, clear the work surface of all clutter—tools, scraps of wood, dust, and so on—then set out your inspirational drawings, paints, brushes, and cloths so that they are close at hand. Now mix the yellow ochre to a good consistency with water, give the carving another quick dust over, then lay on a couple of good well-brushed coats. Allow the paint to dry, then take your graded sandpapers and knock back the color to break the surface. Try to achieve a weathered, worn patina (FIG. 1-8).

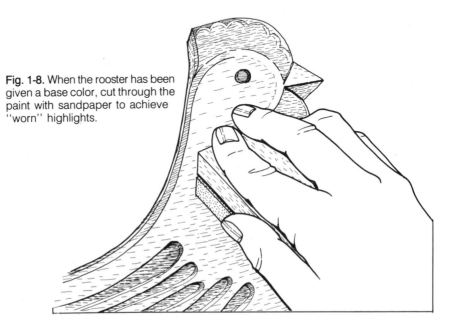

Fig. 1-8. When the rooster has been given a base color, cut through the paint with sandpaper to achieve "worn" highlights.

This done, take a small brush and the mixed and prepared red acrylic, and pick out the comb, the eyes, and the feathers. Finally, when the paint is dry, take the finest of sandpapers and go over the whole work just rubbing back all the corners and sharp edges.

- Our weather-vane sculpture is worked at about half size; that is to say, from tail to beak it measures about 20 inches. If you decided to make a full-size rooster—that is, a bird about 40 inches from tail to beak—then don't forget to double up the wood thickness and use 2-inch material.

- If you intend using this rooster as a weather vane, then it might be as well to protect the wood with a couple of coats of yacht varnish.

- If your friendly blacksmith/car mechanic is going to make you up a weather vane pivot/bearing, specify either sealed bearings or brass.

- As an indoor sculpture, the rooster can be mounted on a ⅜-inch brass rod set in a chunk-wood or log base.

- If you prefer, you might like to give the matte acrylic a clear, antiqued, crackle varnish finish. (Check a paint supplier's catalog.)

CARVING AND PAINTING A
House Signboard IN THE
English Tradition

Fig. 2-1. A sign board with a traditional sun motif. See how the sun has been given character features. You might be able to personalize the design and carve a portrait face, for example.

As to when and where the first signboards were made and used, who can say? All we know is that from ancient times, tradespeople used actual objects, carved and painted pictures of objects, or symbols to advertise their wares (FIG. 2-1). For example, in Roman Britain, a green bush hung outside a building signified that wine was sold there; barber-surgeons in the Middle Ages marked their premises with a blood-red stick or pole bound with bandages; apothecaries hung a pestle and mortar over their door; and so on.

In ages past, when most people were illiterate, it was obviously a good idea to hang easily recognizable pictorial representations outside business premises. Of course, when communities were small, it didn't matter so much that, say, Mr. Jones the saddle-maker made and sold his wares from an unmarked building. Signs only really became important and necessary when communities began to grow in size.

In the first quarter of the seventeenth century, the city of London was so large and sprawling that Charles I declared that all citizens had to hang signs up or over their premises. So it was that by and by the streets of all British cities became a colorful, extravagant riot of carved and painted boards. Old prints and illustrations show city streets absolutely bristling with all manner of boldly carved and vividly colored symbolic imagery.

This state of affairs was fine and completely logical for locals who appreciated that a picture of say a Turk was associated with tobacco, and the sign of a naked boy marked the premises of a coffin maker. One wonders, though, what strangers and travelers made of signs that showed pictures of pineapples, unicorns, golden chains, and the like. Who could guess, for example, that a picture of a cat and herring marked the premises of a perfumers (FIG. 2-2)?

Materials

A slab of 1½-inch-thick white pine wood that measures about 18 inches wide and 24 inches long
A selection of oil or acrylic paints, colors to suit

Tools

A coping saw
A selection of wood-carving tools, including:
A V-tool
A knife
A shallow gouge
A vise
A pencil, ruler, and compass
A rasp
A graded pack of sandpapers
A selection of broad- and fine-pointed brushes
All the usual workshop items, like work-out paper, tracing papers, cloths, and paint tubs.

Fig. 2-2. Inspirational designs—a fish, the traditional golden fleece, a drapers sign, the White Hart inn with bunch of grapes, and a shipwright's axe. See how variously the signs are painted, worked in relief, and carved in the round.

With huge, extravagant, carved, painted, and gilt signs marking every house and business, the eighteenth century might almost be described as the age of the signboard. If the few remaining inn and pub signs are anything to go by, it must have been a wonderfully exuberant sight. By the middle of the eighteenth century, however, trade and house signs were so numerous and large—with some signs bridging streets and blocking pathways—and the designs so obscure that really they failed to fulfill their original purpose. Illustrations of the period show streets overshadowed by signs, signs pulling the fronts off buildings, signs falling and killing passers-by, and so on. In about 1760, another law was passed declaring that all signs had to be removed.

DESIGN AND TECHNIQUE

First take a good look around you and see how signboards are still an important feature of our everyday surroundings. See how although modern "signs" are now printed on paper, cut out of flat plastic, or flashed up on the television, rather than being wood-carved and painted, the imagery is as colorful and symbolic as ever. When you have studied shop and trade signs, then take a slow walk through a rural neighborhood and study as many house signs as possible. See how individuals still enjoy visual puns and imagery "jokes." A Mr. and Mrs. Sharp, might have a pair of carved scissors as a gate sign, or a much-traveled retired couple might have a signboard of a gypsy caravan and the house name "DunRoaming." Next, visit a museum and see if you can find old signs. Certainly look at the whole range, but concentrate on wood-carved and painted primitive folk-made signs that were made before 1900.

On your travels from modern street houseboards to museum exhibits, take a sketchbook and make a series of color, technique and design studies. When you get your sketchbook back to your workshop, settle on one or other of the designs, or use ours (FIG. 2-3), then decide on size. When you have settled on a sign size and worked up a good master design, make a careful tracing.

Finally, take your slab of wood and, bearing in mind that the sign will be deeply carved and painted, that it will be hung outside in all weathers, and so on, check the wood for possible faults. Ideally, when you are choosing your wood, go for a type that is easy to carve, and a piece that is free from large, dead knots, grain twists, stains, end splits, and sappy edges.

Setting Out the Design and Cutting the Blank

When you have taken a tracing from the master design, pencil-press transfer the traced lines through to the working face of the wood. This done, secure the wood in the vise or clamp it to your workbench.

With a coping saw and rasp, rough out the basic, round-topped form. When you have cleared away the waste, take the rasp or a spokeshave or drawknife and, noting the run of the grain, work the curve from side to top. Work the edges and corners and leave the wood looking nicely smooth edged and round cornered. Finally, with the rasp and the pack of graded sandpapers, take all faces of the wood to a good, smooth finish.

Fig. 2-3. Working drawings—the scale is a little over 1 grid square to 1 inch.

Setting in the Design and Lowering the Ground

Make sure that the lines of the design are clearly penciled in. If necessary, label areas *leave*, *waste*, *high relief*, or whatever. Set the wood square on the bench and arrange your selection of tools so that they are comfortably at hand.

Take the V-section tool and very carefully go over the whole design, cutting-in on the waste side or on the pencil-drawn lines (FIG. 2-4). Don't try to cut too deeply; just guide the tool with one hand and push and maneuver with the other.

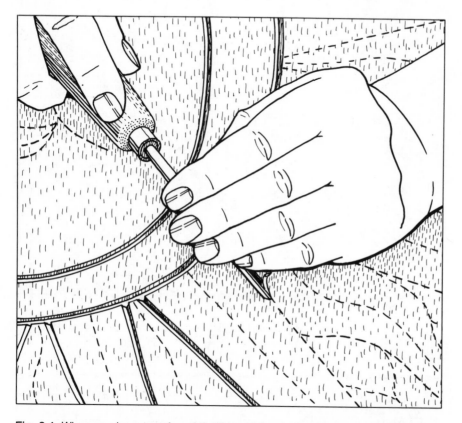

Fig. 2-4. When you have transferred the lines of the design through to the wood, use a V-section tool to cut-in the pencil lines. In the first instance, cut-in to a depth of about ⅛ to ¼ inch.

When you have cut-in a trench that slants slightly away from the design, then take the shallow-curve gouge in both hands and very carefully set about lowering the waste ground (FIG. 2-5). Lower the wood around the "tongues," or rays, of the sun, and between the sun and the face. With one eye on the run of the grain and working with a steady push-and-thrust action of the shallow gouge, gradually lower the waste ground to a depth of about ⅛ to ¼ inch.

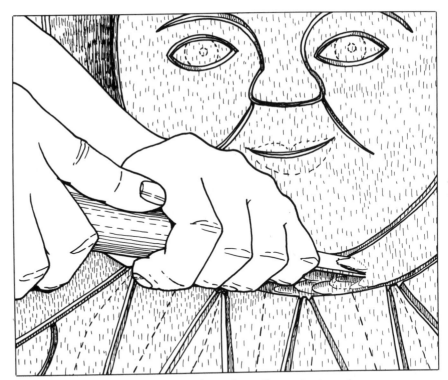

Fig. 2-5. Use the gouge of your choice to lower the waste ground.

Modeling the Form

When you have stepped and lowered the ground to suit, then take a knife or gouge and gently round off all the sharp edges and corners of the high relief.

Now have a look at the working drawings and also your sketches to see how the various high relief areas need to be curved, angled, rounded, and otherwise shaped. Take your chosen tool and feel your way over all the hills and valleys that go to make up the design. Working the board with a slow, but sure, little-by-little approach, remove small, crisp curls of wood. Gradually work closer toward the finished design.

Once you have rounded the main forms, then you can begin to model the tongues of fire. Position your knife on a tongue centerline, then slice at an angle so as to give the tongue its characteristic high-centered sharp-edged shape.

When you come to carve the face, slice out the dipped areas around the nose, cheeks, and lips. Aim to work the features so that the cheeks look full and rounded. Try to emphasize the bulge of the chin and cheeks, and the rather full roundness of the upper eyelids. Once you have established the overall form, take a small pointed knife or a small spoon-bit gouge, and dig out the two eye holes.

Continue, working a slice here, making a scoop there, deepening an area here, trying to emphasize a roundness there. Go backward and forward over the wood, extending and adjusting, until you have what you consider is an exciting form. If you have problems deciding how to make a cut, stop awhile, sort the problem out on a piece of scrap wood, or adjust the design, and then continue as before. Of course, if at any time you get the urge to change the whole design, then go ahead. One of the pleasures of carving a design of this character is the fact that you are free to follow your own flights of fancy.

Cutting the Letters

Have a good look at our working drawings and note how the letterforms are strong, bold, and spontaneous. That is to say, although the letters do have serifs and do look to be formal, traditional, and of a Greek type, really their shape owes more to the direct and simple use of the knife than to any particular formalized letter style.

For starters, take a piece of scrap wood and a good, sharp knife and concentrate your efforts on cutting strong, spontaneous, V-section letterforms. Each letter has its own particular problems. For example, a lowercase e is made up of tight curves, so you need to keep a close watch on the run of the grain; the d has a difficult-to-work linkup, and so on.

If you are a beginner, it might be a good idea to have a practice run with all your chosen letters. When you have worked out the length of the word and the spacing, draw out a full-size master design and pencil-press transfer the letters through to the working face of the wood. Don't worry too much about the small details, such as the precise tail curves of the s and y, but do make sure that the total block of letters is square and well placed.

When you are happy with the placing, hold the knife with a two-handed stabbing action, and make a deep downward cut into the first letter; that is to say, a cut that sets out the centerline of the letter form (FIG. 2-6). In the first instance, cut-in to a depth of about ¼ inch, then angle in toward your initial cut so as to remove a sliver of wood and make a V-section trench or trough (FIG. 2-7). Don't try to cut the full width of the letter at a single stroke, but rather gradually widen and deepen the trough with a series of cuts. And so you work, guiding and controlling the knife with both hands.

If you feel the wood beginning to tear or cut up rough, then stop and adjust the direction of your cut to suit the run of the grain. When you come to carving a cross-over letter—that is, a letter with two crossing members or a junction—then the V-trenches or troughs need to meet so that there is a nicely formed, crisp-edged, triangulated intersection. (See the working drawings and details.) Throughout the letter-cutting stage, be prepared to stop every few minutes or so to study the grain and to sharpen your knives.

PAINTING

When you have worked a signboard with a vigorous motif and good, strong letterforms, clear the work surface of all clutter and dust, and set out all your paints and brushes. Start by making sure that the carved board is completely

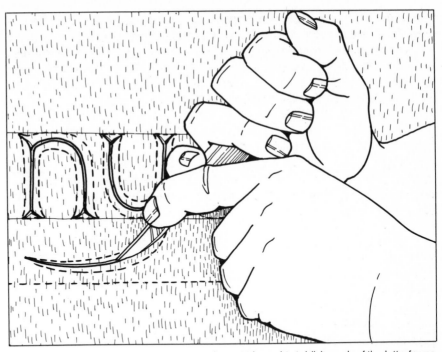

Fig. 2-6. When you begin to work the lettering, cut-in and establish each of the letterforms with a deep central cut.

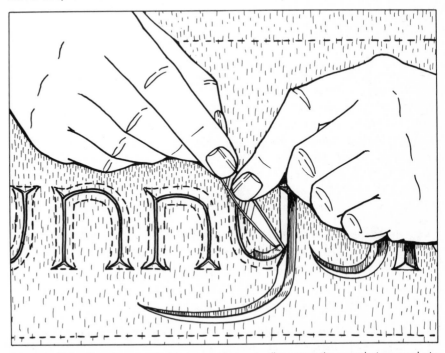

Fig. 2-7. Using the deep central cut as a stop cut, slice away the wood at an angle to make a **V**-section trench.

free from dust and debris. Then, drying and rubbing down between coats, lay on a single undercoat and at least two top glossy coats.

Decide on your letter colors—that is, the color inside the trough—and then paint them in it with a medium fine-point brush. When the trough colors are dry, take your best fine-point brush and a color that contrasts both the ground and the trough colors, and carefully edge-stripe each letter (see FIG. 2-8).

The way you paint your particular carved motif will, of course, relate to the character and the subject of your board. Finally, when you consider the board finished, lay on a well-brushed coat of yacht varnish.

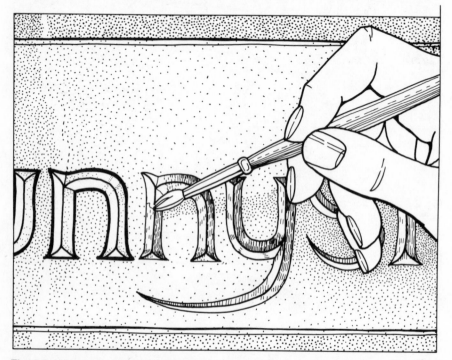

Fig. 2-8. When you have painted in the ground, use a fine-point brush and a contrasting color to pick out the cut letters.

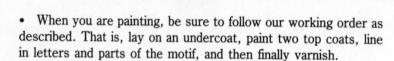

- When you are painting, be sure to follow our working order as described. That is, lay on an undercoat, paint two top coats, line in letters and parts of the motif, and then finally varnish.

- If you want your board to be viewed from both sides, you might consider having a pierced design.

- If you are going to hang the board over a doorway, make sure that the chains/screws are strong.

WHITTLING A
Love Spoon
IN THE
Welsh Tradition

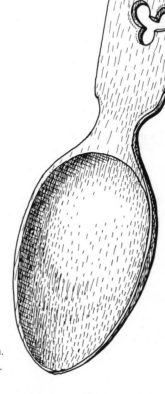

Fig. 3-1. A traditional love spoon form. Note the chain and the pierced motifs.

Welsh love spoons are best described as wooden, knife-carved, nonfunctional, rustic labors of love that were traditionally given as tokens of romantic intent (FIG. 3-1). That is to say, they are little spoon-shaped carvings that really served no useful purpose other than conveying the message "I love you." Illiterate tongue-tied rustics and sailors, intent on getting the message across, would take up a piece of found wood and then proceed to carve the most elaborately decorated and fanciful spoon or spoons. Once made, these spoons were given to sweethearts as a token, much as we might now send a Valentine's card or a box of chocolates. Embellished with carved and incised letters, dates, and symbols of love, these spoons were intended to set the scene for courting. If the spoons were accepted and acknowledged, then at least the poor lovelorn lad knew that his intentions were welcomed.

As to why the Welsh carved spoons, it is thought that either they were intended to be three-dimensional puns on the old English term "to spoon," meaning to indulge in demonstrative lovemaking, or perhaps by giving a spoon shape the lover was saying to his sweetheart that they might, as a married couple, fit together like two well-matched spoons. Some authorities consider that there is a link between making carved love tokens in general and the Anglo-Saxon word *spon*, meaning to chip or splinter.

As for the carved and incised decorations on the spoons, these are rather more obvious: hearts stand for love, little collections of caged balls are taken to symbolize the security and togetherness of love and the desired number of children, rabbits symbolize fertility, shoes stand for marriage, spades and wheels mean "I will work for you," and so on (FIG. 3-2). Love spoons were, by their very nature, extravagant boasts of skill.

Materials

A piece of straight-grained, easy-to-work, knot-free wood that measures about 18x3x2 inches
Furniture wax

Tools

A large sheet of work-out paper
A sheet of tracing paper
A workbench and a vise
A metal ruler
A coping saw
A compass
Two knives: one with a round end and one with a pointed end
A hand drill with a small bit
Pencils, and an oilstone

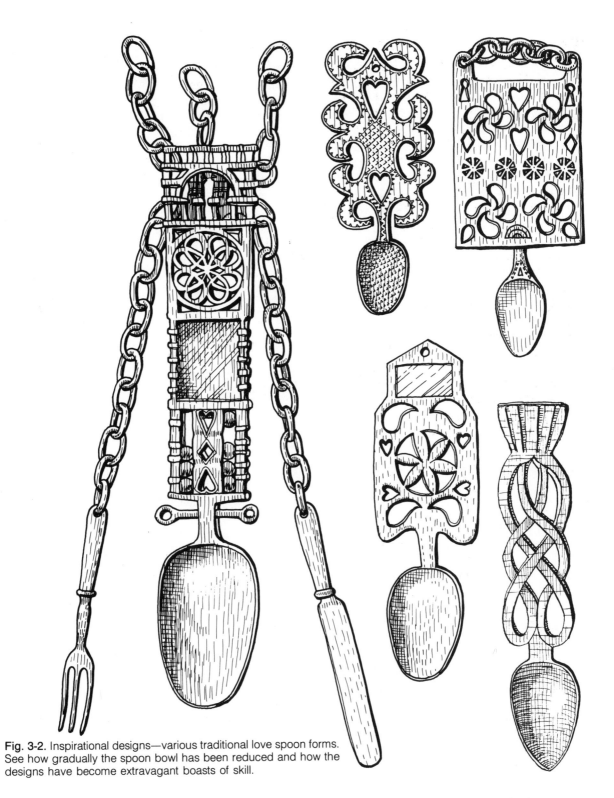

Fig. 3-2. Inspirational designs—various traditional love spoon forms. See how gradually the spoon bowl has been reduced and how the designs have become extravagant boasts of skill.

DESIGN AND TECHNIQUE

First of all, have a good look at the working drawings (FIG. 3-3) and see how the love spoon and the chain have been carved from a single, quite large, piece of easily worked, smooth-grained wood. For example, with the spoon being about 12 inches long and every two links of the chain being worked from about 3 inches of wood, you will need a piece of wood that is at least 18 inches long.

Of course, there's no reason why you shouldn't modify the project and have a smaller spoon or fewer links to the chain. Also have a look at the various inspirational drawings (FIG. 3-2) and see how you might change the design and introduce other motifs, patterns, and symbols.

When you have spent time considering all the possible modifications, then take a sheet of work-out paper and draw the whole project out to size. That is to say, establish the overall form of the spoon, the shape and size of the piercing, the number and size of the chain links, and the shape of the spoon profile. Note how the hexagonal piercing has been set out with the compass.

It might also be as well, at this stage, to visit a folk museum. Try to see Welsh love spoons in particular, and Swedish, German, and Polish love tokens in general.

When you have considered all the design and technique implications of the project, take a piece of scrap wood and have a trial run. Concentrate your efforts on the dishing of the spoon and the chain links. Finally, once you have established all the elevations on the work-out paper and have marked in the areas that need to be wasted, then make a good tracing.

Setting Out the Wood and First Cuts

Once you have made a good tracing, place the wood on the work surface and check it over for faults. Now, take the tracing and pencil-press transfer the traced lines through to the various faces of the wood. Clearly label the spoon and chain profiles.

This done, put the wood in the vise and use the coping saw to clear away the main areas of waste (FIG. 3-4). Clear the wood from all sides of the spoon and from alongside the chain stem. Work one face of the wood at a time, then reestablish the drawn lines and saw out the other profile.

When all the waste has been cleared, have another look at your working drawings, then take a pencil and mark in the primary reference points: the bowl of the spoon, the neck, the position of the decorative hex piercing, and so on. Finally, take a knife and make stop cuts around the neck and at the top of the spoon where the handle meets the chain.

Carving the Handle and the Bowl

When the overall shape has been roughed out, take the round-ended knife and start to cut away the wood from the dish of the spoon. Whittle from side to center, all the while working with tight, thumb-supported paring cuts to remove small, crisp curls of wood (FIG. 3-5).

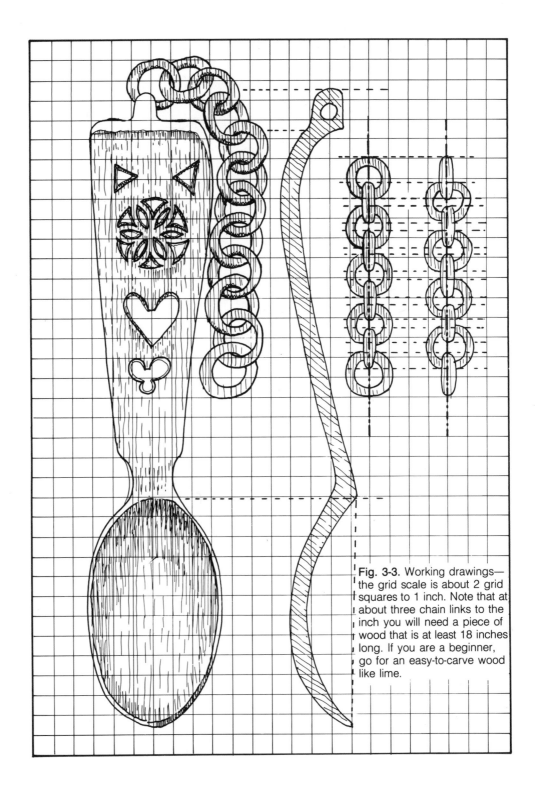

Fig. 3-3. Working drawings—the grid scale is about 2 grid squares to 1 inch. Note that at about three chain links to the inch you will need a piece of wood that is at least 18 inches long. If you are a beginner, go for an easy-to-carve wood like lime.

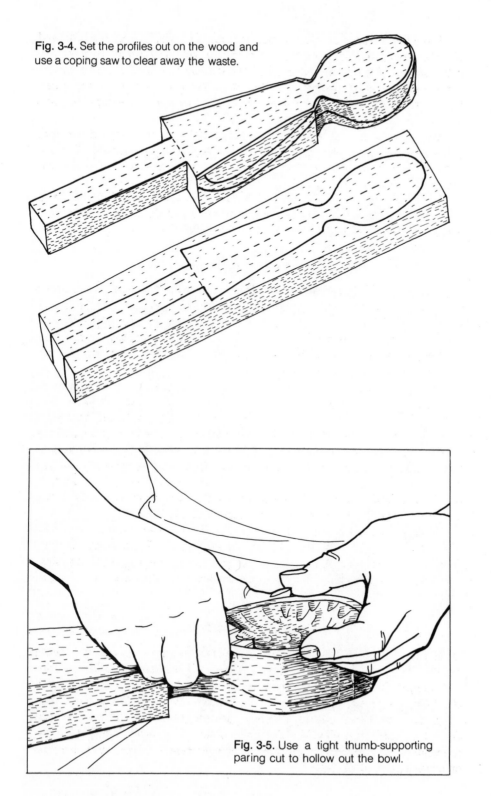

Fig. 3-4. Set the profiles out on the wood and use a coping saw to clear away the waste.

Fig. 3-5. Use a tight thumb-supporting paring cut to hollow out the bowl.

From time to time as you are working, run the calipers over the bowl and take a series of thickness readings. Aim for a wood thickness of about ¼ inch at the center of the dish, and gradually feather up to a bowl rim of about ⅛ inch thick. As you are working, try to cut across or at an angle to the grain, don't be tempted to dig with the knife point, and always use carefully controlled cuts.

When you have achieved a good bowl form, hold the spoon so that the chain end is nearest you, then start to carve and shape the spoon handle. Working from one stop cut to another, establish the sweeping curve of the handle and the delicate neck area.

When you have whittled what you consider to be a well-formed spoon, cradle it in your hand or on your lap, and bring the surface of the wood to a smooth, slightly rippled finish (FIG. 3-6).

Piercing the Handle

Once the spoon has been cut, carved, dished, and brought to a good finish, start the delicate piercing operation. First check with the working drawings that all is correct and as described, then pencil-press transfer the lines of the various pierced motifs through to the surface of the spoon. That is to say, mark in the position of the hex roundel, the heart, the shape under the heart, and the two little triangles.

Now secure the wood in the vise, and use the hand drill to work pilot holes through all the areas that are to be pierced. Unhitch the coping-saw blade, pass it through one of the pilot holes, fix the blade back in the saw frame, then start to fret out the motif window. Noting the delicate areas of short grain and the need to angle the saw blade so that it is piercing the wood at 90 degrees to the working face, gently saw and pierce each motif window (FIG. 3-7). As you pierce the wood, try to keep to the waste side of the drawn lines. Continue, unhitching the saw blade, maneuvering the wood in the vise, and generally sawing away at a steady pace until you have pierced all the motifs.

Finally, take the wood from the vise, cradle the spoon in one hand, take the knife in the other, and work all the raw sawn edges. Work with a carefully controlled thumb-paring action. Never cut with great sweeping hacking strokes, but rather work little by little, all the while removing delicate, crisp curls of wood.

Cutting the Chain

Once you have cleared the waste from the chain end of the spoon, you should be left with a long stem of wood that is about 1 x 1 inch in section. With a ruler and a pencil, divide each long side of the wood into three parts. Now draw parallel lines along the length of the wood and across the ends. If you now cross-hatch the outer two-thirds on each face, you should be left with a white strip down the center of each side and a white cross on the sawn end. Noting that the white wood needs to be left, take a knife and remove all the cross-hatched or shaded areas (FIG. 3-8).

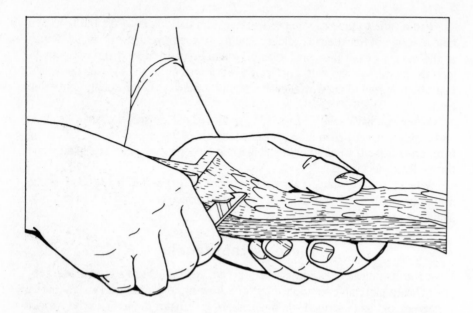

Fig. 3-6. When you are working the handle, hold the spoon so that the chain end is nearest to you. Use the knife to work delicate shaving cuts.

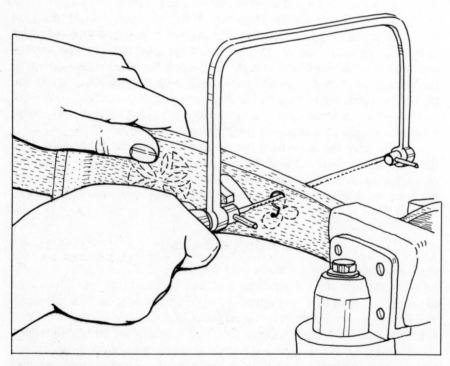

Fig. 3-7. Drill starter or pilot holes and then use a coping saw to fret out the holes. Hold the saw so that the blade is 90 degrees to the working face of the wood.

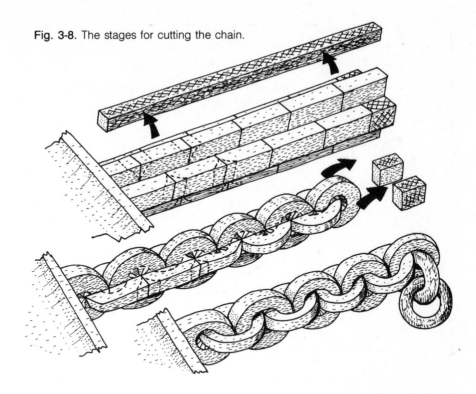

Fig. 3-8. The stages for cutting the chain.

When you have done this, have another look at the working drawings and then take a pencil and set out the position of the chain links, as illustrated in FIG. 3-8. When you have established a long stem of wood that is cross-shaped in section, take a knife and work stop cuts between each of the links. Now shape and enlarge each of the cuts to establish a rough chain profile. This done, work the stop cuts deeper and deeper until they begin to pierce the center of the links.

Next, looking at one face or plane, select two touching links and little by little carve and work the wood between them until you manage to pierce the eye of the link that holds them together. When you reach a point where you have removed most of the waste wood in and around the links, take your smallest, sharpest, most pointed knife, and gently nibble away at the last little bridges of wood that hold the links together. As each link is cut free, tidy it up with a few swift strokes, and then move on to the next one.

Finally, take the whole project to a good, smooth, rounded finish by clearing away all the burrs and rough edges. Give the wood a swift rub down with furniture wax and a fluff-free cloth.

- If you are a beginner, it might be as well to start by making a trial three-link chain with a scrap of wood.

(. . . continued)

- With a project of this character, it is most important that your knives be razor sharp. To this end, spend time honing the blades on the oilstone. (See the *Workshop Data* section.)

- Choose your wood with care. Go for a smooth-grained, easy-to-work white wood. Lime, white pine, holly, and fruit wood are all suitable.

CARVING A *Tulip Panel* IN THE *English Jacobean Flat-Relief Tradition*

Fig. 4-1. Note how the design is symmetrical and see how all the forms relate to tulip motifs.

In the early sixteenth century, tulips were introduced into the Low Countries from Constantinople. By about 1637, they were so popular that they became the subject of an extraordinary speculation known as *tulipmania*. There was a time when prices for a single bulb rose to as much as 2,600 guilders. And so it was that in the seventeenth century, the cult of the tulip swept Holland, England, Germany, and of course America.

The tulip motif appears on all manner of items—on pottery, on painted furniture, on embroideries, and perhaps most interesting of all, on carved furniture and fittings (FIG. 4-1). Known variously as *low-relief, flat-relief, strapwork*, and *Jacobean*, the wood carvings of this period are characterized by being flat faced, sharp edged, unmodeled, smooth lined, symmetrical, and wasted so that the motifs give the appearance of being raised up from a sunken ground. The lowered or sunken ground is not generally cut away to any great depth, usually no more than between ⅛ to ¼ inch, but it is always worked so that both the motifs in relief and the ground look to be evenly, almost mechanically, carved.

As to how the tulip motif occurs in the context of sixteenth and seventeenth flat-relief strapwork, more often than not the flower has been conventionalized, so that although it does not seem to have much in common with the natural article, nevertheless, it has all the essential characteristics. For example, with the project design, the primary central form is tulip shaped; the little details within the main form draw their inspiration from tulips; the leaves that branch out from the central stem are tulips in profile; and even the forms that spring out from all the secondary tuliplike flowers are in themselves tulip shaped.

The floral designs and motifs that occur on English and American chest panels of this period are not so much realistic, naturalistic, wood-carved interpretations of the tulip, but rather they have been reduced to powerful, strident, primitive, abstracted forms that have all the intrinsic features and contain the fundamental essence of the species *Tulipa Liliaceace*.

Materials

A 1-inch-thick slab of quarter-sawn, half-seasoned oak that measures about 24x12 inches
Linseed oil
Beeswax polish

Tools

A large shallow-curve gouge
A small shallow-curve gouge
A V-section straight tool
A spoon gouge
A flat-bent tool and a dog-leg chisel
A mallet
A small hammer
A punch

(. . . continued)

Fig. 4-2. Inspirational designs—a selection of traditional tulip-based designs. See how the motifs are flat faced and unmodeled, and how the sunken ground is punch textured.

A C-clamp or bench holdfast
Work-out paper
Tracing paper
Pencils
A metal rule
A brush
A stout workbench or table

DESIGN AND TECHNIQUE

Start this project by visiting a stately home or a museum. Focus your attention on large oak chests, coffers, and Bible boxes that were made in England and America between say 1630 and 1700. Study all the panel and running border designs and motifs, and see how many of them relate to, or are inspired by, tulips and tuliplike flowers. Note how the designs tend nearly always to be symmetrical and worked in flat relief (FIG. 4-2). Study especially the beautiful uncomplicated directness of the carved forms, and see how the carver has achieved a nice balance between the raised relief, or *plateau wood,* of the motif and the sunken, wasted wood that is the lowered ground.

When you have run your eyes and hands over examples of such work, then select a single characteristic panel or detail and make a series of analytical sketches. Take note of all the main features, as described. Along the way, see also how, although the carvers of the period worked towards symmetrical patterns and motifs, they never pushed or forced a design. For example, if on a Bible box or chest there needed to be an asymmetrical feature like dates and initials, then the carver was quite happy to balance the design with an extra floral flourish. By aiming for symmetry and yet at the same time feeling free enough to let the design grow and develop, the carvers were able to achieve designs that to our eyes look to be natural, informal, and perfectly understated.

When you have studied a number of flat-relief tulip designs and you have a good understanding of just how they have been designed, worked, and carved, then take all your study material back to the workshop and decide how you want your design to be. Are you going to copy our design directly (FIG. 4-3), or are you going to make modifications? Draw the design up to size and make a good tracing. Note that, with a design of this shape and character, you need only draw out one-half of the motif.

Preparing the Wood

When you have worked what you consider is a good characteristic design, then pin your inspirational material up around your working area and set out your tools and materials so that they are comfortably at hand. This done, have a good look at your slab of oak and make sure that it is free from splits, loose and dead knots, and spongy or sappy edges.

Fig. 4-3. Working drawing—the grid scale is about 2 squares to 1 inch.

Take your large scoop gouge and swiftly go over the working face of the wood, bringing it to good order; that is to say, leave the wood looking smooth and dappled. Don't think of this stage as being a cosmetic exercise. It is much better to see it as setting the pace and mood for all that is to follow. This being so, take your time and try to enjoy the feel and character of the oak.

When the wood has been prepared, establish a centerline, and then pencil-press transfer the lines of the traced design through to the working face of the wood. Finally, take a soft pencil and shade in all the areas that need to be cut away and wasted. If necessary, make pencil notes on the wood and label areas.

Setting In

When the design has been clearly set out, secure the wood to the bench with the clamp or holdfast, then take the V-tool and start to set-in the design by cutting a V-section trench or groove on the waste side of your drawn lines (FIG. 4-4). Don't try to cut away too much wood; just follow the lines with the tool and lower the wood little by little until you have achieved a ¼-inch-deep groove that stands clear of the drawn lines by about ⅛ inch. Bear in mind that you will, at times, be cutting both with and across the grain. Don't force the tool, but rather be prepared to approach the cut from different directions, and be ready to modify your angle of cut if the wood starts to cut up ragged or rough.

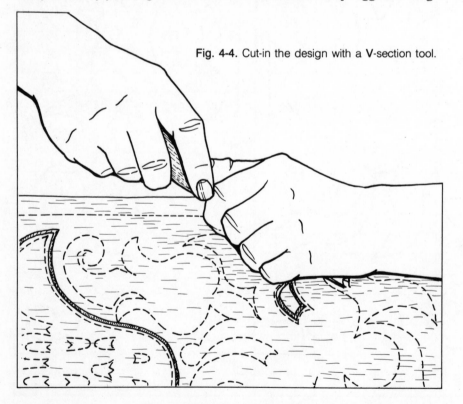

Fig. 4-4. Cut-in the design with a V-section tool.

When you have established the design with a V-section groove, then take one or other of your U-section tools and start setting in or chopping in along the actual drawn lines of the design (FIG. 4-5). Hold the tool so that its handle is at an angle over the motif and then chop-in with little taps of the mallet. The wood between the drawn line and the V-trench will crumble away. Working in this way, go around the whole motif, establishing the characteristic vertical-cut, sharp-faced profile, and the depth of the lowered ground.

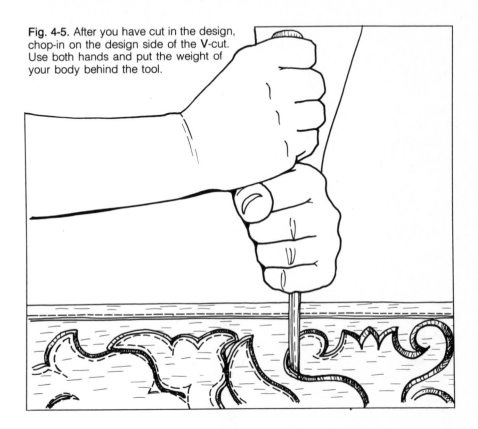

Fig. 4-5. After you have cut in the design, chop-in on the design side of the V-cut. Use both hands and put the weight of your body behind the tool.

Wasting the Ground

When you have set-in the design, take your selection of scoop chisels and gouges, and start to cut away the ground (FIG. 4-6). Be careful that you don't rip the wood up in great chunks. Just work with short, controlled, shallow scooping cuts.

If, as you are working, the wood cuts rough or the tool looks to be smashing through the wood, rather than swiftly and smoothly cutting, then try approaching the grain from another angle. If this fails, stop awhile and spend time bringing the tool to a keen edge with the oilstone.

Continue, lowering the whole ground area to a depth of about ¼ inch. Don't aim for a completely smooth finish; just clear away the waste and sharpen the angle between the flat-relief wood and the ground.

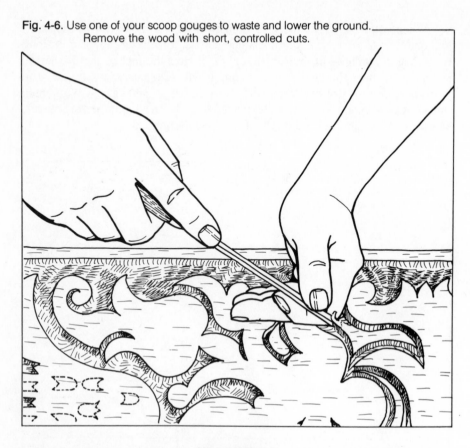

Fig. 4-6. Use one of your scoop gouges to waste and lower the ground. Remove the wood with short, controlled cuts.

FINISHING

If you have another look at your inspirational material and our working designs, you will see that although many carvers of this period did *round-up* their designs—that is to say, they cut off all the sharp edges and then went on to model the flowers—in this particular instance, the motifs are left completely flat faced, apart from a few swift scoop cuts (FIG. 4-7).

Once you have chopped in and scoop-carved the dozen or so very swift cuts that decorate the head of the main flower, then take the flat-bent tool and tidy up the whole of the lowered ground. Don't overwork the wood; just aim to leave it so that it looks to be clean and efficiently cut.

Now take the punch and the hammer, make sure that the wood is cushioned and firmly supported, then go over the whole of the sunken ground punching in the mechanical texture (FIG. 4-8). Again, don't fuss around, just work the wood with swift efficiency.

Finally, brush out all the nooks and crannies. Make sure that the panel is free from burrs and rough areas. Then rub on linseed oil and beeswax, and burnish to a smooth finish.

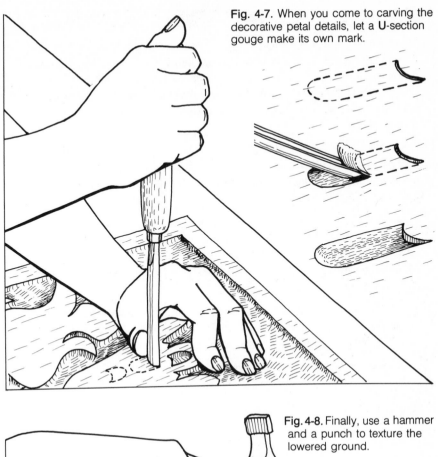

Fig. 4-7. When you come to carving the decorative petal details, let a **U**-section gouge make its own mark.

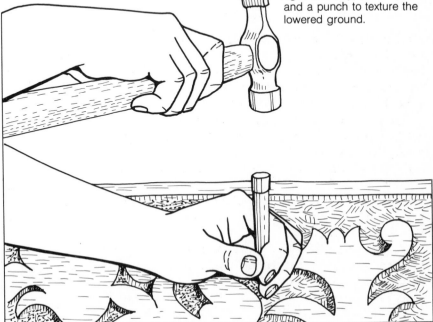

Fig. 4-8. Finally, use a hammer and a punch to texture the lowered ground.

• When you are wasting the ground, be careful that you don't catch and damage parts of the motif that are short grained and fragile. For example, when you are clearing the ground in and around the rather narrow valleys between the main stem and the tulip branches, take it slowly. If necessary work with smaller, more sympathetic tools.

• With a carving of this character, the success or failure of the design hinges not so much on the design being imaginative or daring as on the motifs being bold, vigorous, and efficiently cut. Bear this in mind if you decide to adjust or modify the design.

• Although we have suggested the gouges to use for certain steps, always use the tool of your choice. For example, if you prefer working with a spoon gouge rather than the dog-leg, and if you find that it does the job, then it follows that this tool is the best for the task in hand.

• We suggest you use quarter-sawn oak, but again if you would prefer to use lime, walnut, or whatever, then go ahead. Still avoid wood that looks to be knotty, split, or in any way substandard.

MAKING A *Whirligig* IN THE *English and American Tradition*

Fig. 5-1. A traditional whirligig design. See how the form is achieved with the minimum of cuts and fussy details. Go for strong, bold primary colors.

Whirligigs are a sort of hybrid between windmills and weather vanes (FIG. 5-1). They are made of wood, and carved and painted in the form of little figures with flailing arms—boys with bats, fishermen with paddles, soldiers with flags and such like. Not so long ago in rural areas, whirligigs were a relatively common sight. Mounted on rooftops and on the top of poles and shop signs, these figures were designed, with their dancing, turning, spinning antics, to gladden the eye and lighten the heart.

Very little is on record about these comical examples of folk art, other than that they were known to exist in Europe and America as early as the beginning of the eighteenth century. Of course, it's certain that they would have been made and used in wood-carving countries like Switzerland and Germany well before that date.

The name *whirligig* comes from two ancient Norse words: *hvirla* or *wirbil*, meaning to turn about, and *gig* or *giga*, meaning to totter or spin like a top. In America, especially in coastal areas, whirligigs have long been used as wind speed and direction indicators. In England, however, although whirligigs were once a common item, it is thought that they were originally made and used as large silent Sunday toys, or even, in some instances, as silent bird scarers. In the context of this book, whirligigs are knife-worked, whittled and painted, sculptural, animated, kinetic, adult toys.

Materials

A quantity of easily carved wood like lime; for a full-size whirligig:
1 piece of 4x4 inches at 16 inches long
2 blocks at 3x3x3 inches
2 slats 2x¼ inches at 9 inches long
A brass rod ³/₁₆ inch in diameter and 4 inches long
Two washers to fit the rod
A metal rod ¼ inch in diameter and 8 inches long
Acrylic paints, colors to suit
Yacht varnish
Resin glue

Tools

A couple of whittling knives
A small hand drill
A ¼-inch-diameter drill bit
Sandpaper
Work-out paper
Pencils
Brushes
Workshop items like a hacksaw, a coping saw, and paint tubs

Fig. 5-2. Inspirational designs

Soldier, American
Museum In Britain,
16 inches high,
c.1860.

New England Soldier,
22 inches high,
c.1850-1860

Army signalman,
Mount Vernon,
19 inches high,
c.1861

Quaker,
29½ inches high,
c.1875

DESIGN AND TECHNIQUE

First have a good look at the various inspirational designs (FIG. 5-2) and the working drawings (FIG. 5-3). With a whittled project of this size, type, and character, it is necessary to concentrate on the main planes and forms. There are very few fussy areas; just direct, swift knife cuts.

From the toe to the top of the propeller arm or paddle, the whirligig stands about 18 inches high. Now of course if you want to make a much smaller figure then all you do is reduce the scale of the working drawings accordingly. (See the *Workshop Data* section.)

Study the shape and form of the paddle arms, and see how the brass rod is a loose fit in the body and a tight resin-glue fit in the shoulders/paddle arms. The whole figure is painted and varnished and then pivot-mounted on a stout metal rod. The simplest and most direct method of pivot mounting is to drill a hole in the base of the figure and also in the post or whatever, and then to pivot-mount the figure on the post with a length of greased metal rod.

If you are a beginner, it might be as well to have a trial run. Take a much smaller piece of wood and whittle yourself a small maquette. Working in this way, it is possible to sort out all the problems before they actually occur.

When you have considered all the combinations and variations of form, material, and technique, then take a trip to the nearest folk-art museum and see as many examples of whirligigs as possible. When you have seen the many exciting designs and forms, then take a work-out pad and make a series of study sketches.

Finally, when you have considered all the tool, material, and technique implications of the project, and you have decided in your own mind just how you want your whirligig to be, then make a full-size master drawing. Also set out a materials list; that is, decide on type of wood and paint colors, etc.

Setting Out the Design and First Cuts

After you have cut your wood down to size and checked it over for faults, take a tracing from the master design and then pencil-press transfer the traced lines through to the working face of the wood. Make sure that the transferred lines are well established, then shade in all the areas that need to be chopped out and wasted.

Take note of the main features—the nose, the heaviness of the figure, the jaunty uniform, and so on—then take a knife and chop out all the waste (FIG. 5-4). When you have worked the wood in side profile, then make stop cuts around the neck, under the nose, etc. Now cut straight down into the grain, and make angled paring cuts into the stop cuts (FIG. 5-5). In this way, establish the shape of the neck, the proud rounded chest, the jutting chin and nose, and all the other characteristic features.

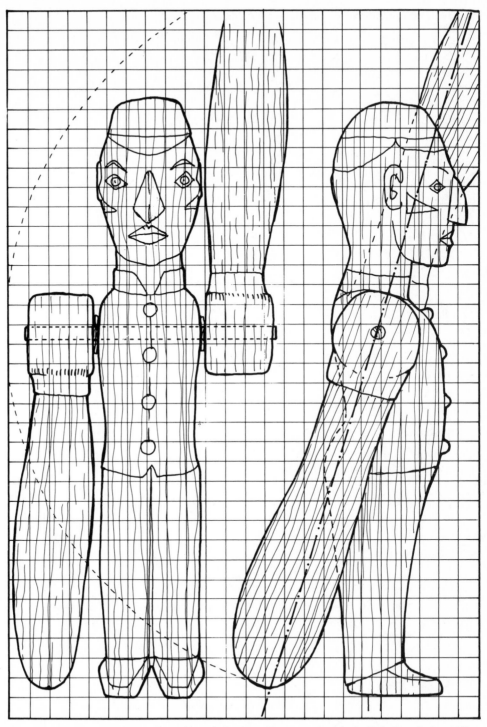

Fig. 5-3. Working drawings—the grid scale is about 2 squares to 1 inch. Note the placing of the brass rod, and see how there are washers between the body and the arms.

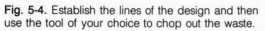

Fig. 5-4. Establish the lines of the design and then use the tool of your choice to chop out the waste.

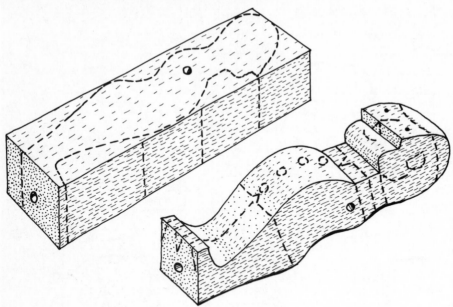

Fig. 5-5. Make stop cuts, then carve and shape the wood using the stop cuts as guides. Be careful that the knife doesn't slip and run away into the grain.

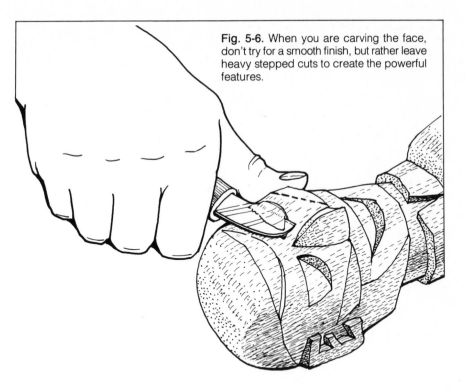

Fig. 5-6. When you are carving the face, don't try for a smooth finish, but rather leave heavy stepped cuts to create the powerful features.

Whittling the Face

Have a good look at the working drawing and details, and see that the face is, in fact, made up of a series of rather bold and direct cuts (FIG. 5-6). Now hold the figure in one hand and the knife in the other, and whittle as if you are going to pare an apple. Make stop cuts at nose, chin, and brow, and then cut at an angle into the stop cuts. Gradually work toward the finish figure.

You will find, as you are working, that actually cutting the wood is much easier than describing how the cuts ought to be made. As with all the other projects, when you become confident, then go your own way. However, continue making well-considered, direct, bold cuts until you have established the heavy stepped profile and the general stance.

Cutting and Making the Paddle Arms

Put the figure to one side, and set out the two shoulder blocks and the two paddle-arm slats. At the making stage, you need to build two identical paddle arms. It's only when they are mounted on the pivot that they become mirror images, or reversed in relation to each other (FIG. 5-7).

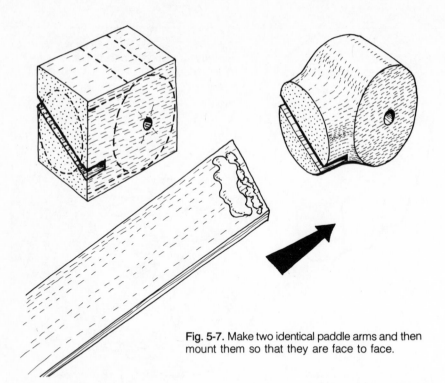

Fig. 5-7. Make two identical paddle arms and then mount them so that they are face to face.

Start by marking out and drilling the pivotal holes. Then take your coping saw, see how the paddle blades are set across the diagonal of the wood, and then cut the slots accordingly. Now take the two ¼-inch-thick slats of wood, draw out the rather round-nosed paddle-blade profile, and then shave and shape the wood to size and fit. Aim for two identical blades, blades that are graded from center to side. The grading needs to run from about ¼ inch thick at the center to about ⅛ inch thick at the edges.

When you have shaved and shaped the two paddle blades, then smear the tenon ends with resin glue, and slide them into the shoulder-slot mortices. The fit needs to be firm, but not so tight that you split the shoulder blocks. If necessary, also drill and pin the blades.

PAINTING

When you have cut and worked both the figure and the paddle-blade arms, then take the wood to a good finish. Don't be tempted to use sandpaper; it is much better to go over all the surfaces with a sharp knife and to leave the wood looking smooth, crisp, and with a tool-marked finish.

Next, have a look at our working drawings, take note of how the colors need to be worked in relation to each other, and then set out your brushes, paint tubs, and the selection of colors. Before you start painting, wipe up all the wood dust with a damp cloth, and then to work. Lay on the main blocks of color—say red for the jacket, black for the hat and so on (see the captions).

When the main ground colors are dry, then use a fine-point brush and contrasting colors to pick out all the little details—the buttons, the trouser stripes, the hat, etc.—and then put the work to one side to dry.

When the acrylic paints are completely dry, give the three units that go to make up the whirligig at least two coats of yacht varnish. When the varnish has dried and you are sure that there are no blobs or tacky lumps, then be ready with the short length of brass rod, the washers, and the resin glue. First clean out the body pivotal hole, make sure that the brass rod slides through the body and is a loose fit, then put the body and washers together in the correct "sandwich" order, as illustrated in FIG. 5-8. When you are happy that all is correct, then dribble a little resin glue into the shoulder holes, and tap the shoulders onto the rod. Finally, drill a hole up through the base of the figure, grease and fit the metal base rod, and the job is done.

Fig. 5-8. When the figure and the paddle blades have been painted, glue-fix the arms to the brass rod so that one is up and the other down. Be sure to use resin glue.

- With a whittled project of this size and character, most of the cuts need to be made with a strong thumb-pushing paring action. This being so, it is most important that the knife is very sharp.

- If the wood cuts up rough or ragged, then either your wood is damp or ill chosen, or your knife needs to be resharpened.

- If your knife slips and you hack off the carving's nose or ear, then just improvise and modify the design accordingly.

- If possible, use brass, rather than iron, for all pivotal parts.

- When you are choosing your wood, it is best to go for smooth, white, even-grained, knot-free types. Reject stuff that looks to be split or resinous.

PROJECT 6

MAKING A
Stencilled and Painted Checker Board
IN THE
American Folk Tradition

Fig. 6-1. The board is both painted and stencil printed. See how the leaf-and-ribbon motif has been reverse- printed. Use bright primary colors.

When the European settlers left their homelands to build new lives in the American wilderness, they couldn't afford any imported luxuries like carpets, wallpapers, and pictures. These ingenious rural folk, spurred on by their need for color and pattern, and inspired by memories of "back home" interiors, soon improvised and developed their own decorative folk crafts. One such craft was that of stenciling (FIG. 6-1). With the settlers each relating to their own particular art and craft traditions—rosemaling from Sweden and Norway, fractur painting from Germany and Switzerland, canal-boat art from England, and so on— stenciling, perhaps more than any other craft, quickly came to characterize the uniquely beautiful, vigorous, multicultural style that we now know as "country rustic," "kitchen hearth," or "American folk."

In the eighteenth and early nineteenth century, as substitutes for wallpapers, murals, overmantel pictures, and carpets, itinerant stencilers and painters traveled around the countryside decorating walls, floors, and furniture with all manner of friezes, borders, and repeat patterns (FIG. 6-2). Working with basic, easily found materials like oiled card, handmade brushes, and paints made from earth colors and milk, the stencilers favored simple, bold, dramatic patterns and motifs. Leaf-and-flower running borders, urns full of flowers, roses, shells, tassels, swags, bells, eagles, flags, doves, foliage, and stylized ribbons were all worked into powerful primitive designs.

As to when and where the first stencil-decorated games board came to be made: maybe there was a tabletop that needed decorating and a stenciler who had some paints left over. Who knows?

Materials

A square piece of prepared white, smooth-grained, knot-free
1-inch-thick plank wood that measures about 16½x16½ inches
A couple of large sheets of stencil plate card
Acrylic paints, colors to suit
A bottle of India ink

Tools

Work-out paper
Tracing paper
A pack of graded sandpapers
A cutting board
A fine-point scalpel
A ruler
A metal straightedge
A selection of paintbrushes
A roll of masking tape
A stencil brush
A sketch pad
Workshop tools, like pencils, old cloths, and newspapers

Fig. 6-2. Inspirational designs—a selection of traditional stencil-printed motifs. Note the strong forms and the color interchange.

DESIGN AND TECHNIQUE

Have a good, long look at the working drawing grids (FIGS. 6-3 and 6-4) and note the 1½-x-1½-inch size of the checkerboard squares. See also how the board has a traditional stylized flower print at each corner, and stylized leaf-and-ribbon prints along each side. As you run your eyes over the design, see how by printing and reversing the leaf-and-ribbon stencil plate it is possible to achieve a centered mirror-image effect. Note also how the whole design has been achieved with just three colors. That is to say, the board has been painted a thin, grain-enhancing yellow, while the checker squares and the flower motifs have been worked in red and black.

It might be helpful to visit a folk or craft museum to see examples of American stenciling. Try if possible to see the work of such notables as Moses Eaton c. 1825, and Henry O. Goodrich c. 1814. If you do get to see these works, make a series of design sketches, and in so doing try to analyze the various pattern compositions, the layouts, the type and number of stencil plates used, and the order of printing.

Next, see how, in this project, the checkerboard grid has been set out with scored lines, the squares of the grid have been hand painted, and each motif has been worked with two stencil plates. When you have a clear understanding of the techniques and the order of work, then sit down with a ruler, pencil, and a sketchbook, and draw up your own design. Finally, when you have achieved a good workable design, then draw it out to size, establish the colors, and make a good tracing.

Preparing the Ground, Scoring the Grid, and Painting the Checker Squares

When you have worked out the size of your board, the placement of the various stenciled motifs, and the order of working, then set your wood out on the work surface and check it over to make sure that it is free from splits, twists, dead knots, and areas of sticky resinous grain. When you have made all these checks, rub the wood down with the graded sandpapers until all surfaces are completely smooth.

The preparation done, take your chosen ground paint, mix a thin wash, and then, with a long-haired mop-type brush, lay on a single coat. Paint all faces of the wood. Keep it thin so that the grain is clearly visible. Once the paint has dried, take the finest sandpaper and swiftly rub down the board to remove burrs and raised grain fibers.

Next, clear the work surface of all clutter, and arrange all your tools so that they are close at hand. Now very carefully mark out the grid with a ruler and a pencil. Double-check to make sure that all is correct. When you are absolutely sure that all the marks are just right, then take a metal straightedge and a razor-sharp scalpel, and score in the decorative grid and the checkerboard lines (FIG. 6-5 shown on page 73). Noting the double-line design feature, work each line with two slightly angled strokes of the scalpel. Try to cut clean V-section trenches. Continue until the whole grid has been marked out.

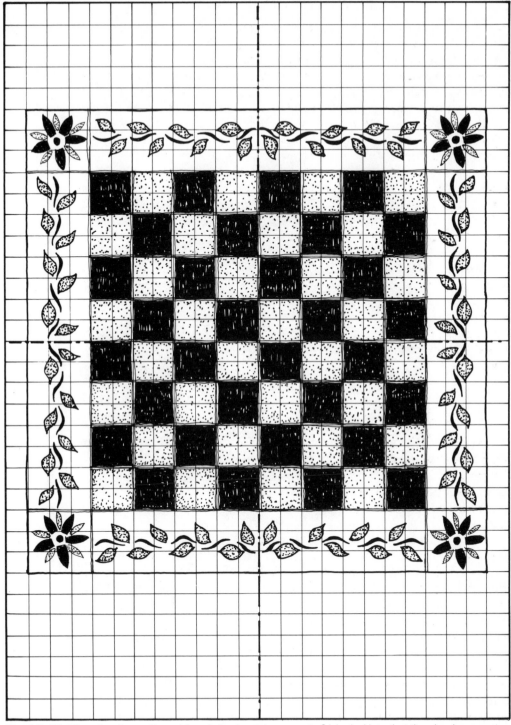

Fig. 6-3. Working drawings—the grid scale is about 1 square to ¾ inch. Note that the checker squares are 1½ × 1½ inches.

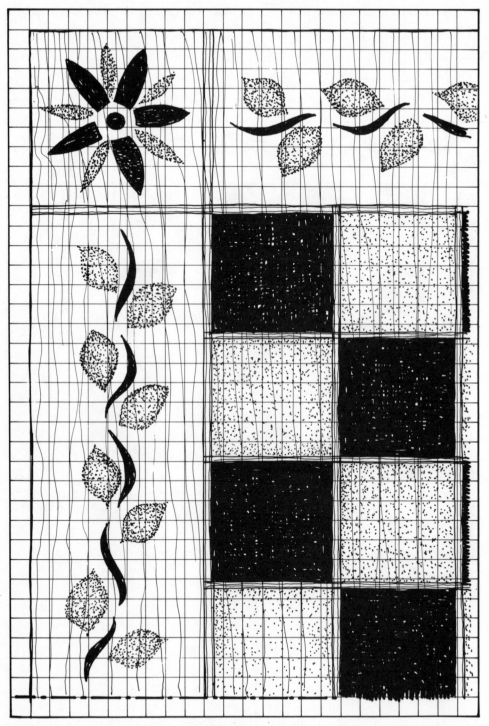

Fig. 6-4. Detail of stenciling. Draw out the grid and use a metal straightedge to score in the checkerboard lines. The cut lines act as paint stops, meaning they contain and control the wet paint.

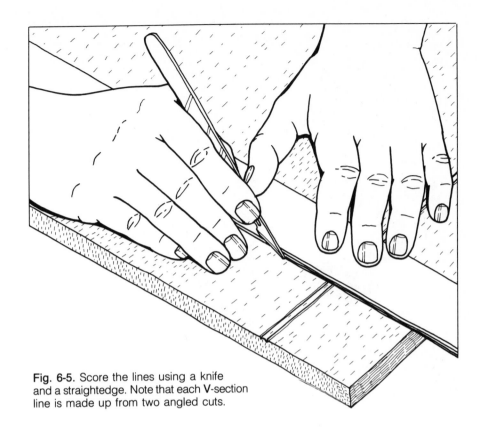

Fig. 6-5. Score the lines using a knife
and a straightedge. Note that each **V**-section
line is made up from two angled cuts.

This done, choose your two checker colors, make sure that your fine-point
brushes are clean, then block in the appropriate squares. If all is correct and
as described, you will find that the incised grid lines act as stop cuts; that is,
they will help to control the flow of the paint (FIG. 6-6 shown on page 74). Finally,
once the paint is dry, take the fine sandpaper and swiftly run it over the wood
to remove all the burrs.

Cutting the Stencil Plates

Take your tracings, break the motifs down into their various colors, then start
to pencil-press transfer the traced lines of the design through to your sheets
of stencil plate card. With this project, you need four completely separate stencil
plates: one for the border ribbon, one for the border leaves, and two for the
alternate petals that go to make up the four corner motifs.

When you have transferred the various elements of the design through to
the stencil card, go over the transferred lines with a pen and ink, then block
in the "windows" of the design with India ink. That is, block in the areas that
are to be cut away.

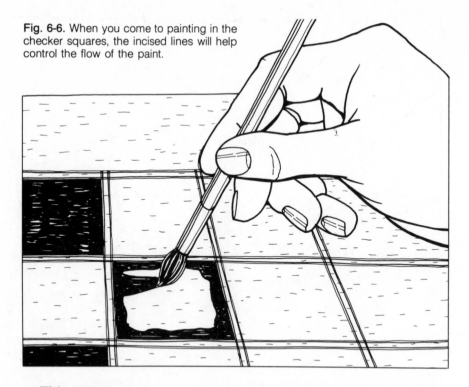

Fig. 6-6. When you come to painting in the checker squares, the incised lines will help control the flow of the paint.

Wait awhile for the ink to dry, have another last checkup just to make sure that all is correct, then start cutting. In working, support the stencil plate on the cutting board and aim to cut through the card with single, clean strokes. All the cut edges need to be free from ragged edges and burrs. To this end, hold and guide the card with one hand, and draw the scalpel toward you and along the lines of the design with the other (FIG. 6-7). Try to manipulate and turn the card so that the scalpel blade is always presented with the line of next cut. NOTE: if you study traditional designs, you will see that they are nearly always worked so that they are made up of easy-to-cut curves.

STENCIL PRINTING

Clear away all the clutter and set out your chosen paints and the stencil brushes. Now, having decided on the order of printing, position the first stencil plate. Make sure that it is perfectly aligned with the edges of the board and the various lines of the scored registration grid, then secure it with tabs of masking tape (FIG. 6-8). This done, dip the brush in the thickish dry-mix paint, and carefully dab in the stencil-plate windows with a series of well-placed up-and-down strokes (FIG. 6-9).

Continue placing and fixing the stencil plates, dabbing in the windows of the design, carefully lifting up the plate, cleaning both sides of the stencil, waiting for the paint to dry, fixing the next stencil plate, and so on, until the whole design has been printed.

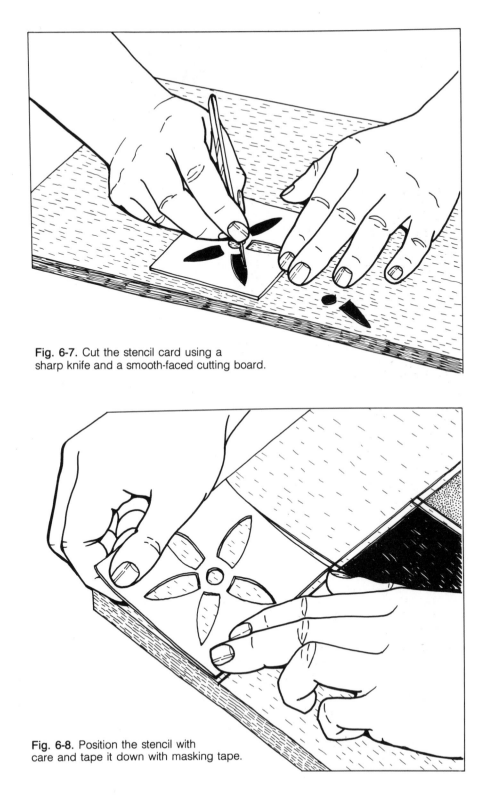

Fig. 6-7. Cut the stencil card using a
sharp knife and a smooth-faced cutting board.

Fig. 6-8. Position the stencil with
care and tape it down with masking tape.

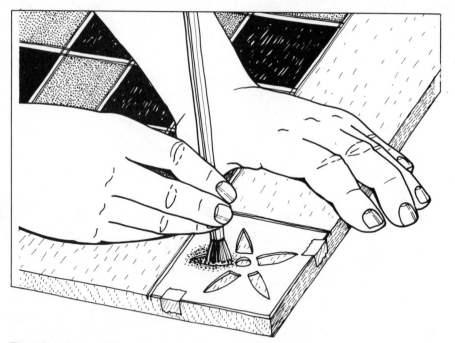

Fig. 6-9. Using a stiff brush, push the paint through the stencil card windows. Work with a dabbing up-and-down action.

- This project uses acrylic paints because they are quick drying; however, you might try using traditional milk paints. You can make them by mixing dry powder colors with skimmed milk powder and water. For an authentic effect go for muted colors, blues, greens, and basic earth browns.

- When you are cutting the stencil plates, work on a smooth, densely surfaced cutting board, such as a sheet of plate glass or hardboard.

- After each and every printing, wipe both sides of the stencil plate with a damp cloth.

- Game boards of this character were often hung on the wall like a picture. To this end your board might have a couple of hanging holes along one edge, or a single corner hole.

- We have chosen in this project to stencil a slab of plank wood. You might, of course, modify the project and print on a sheet of plywood or perhaps on a tabletop.

- If you prefer, you can stencil the checker squares with a carefully cut and considered stencil plate.

PROJECT 7

CARVING A *Biscuit Mold* IN THE *Pennsylvainia Dutch Springerle Board Tradition*

Fig. 7-1. A traditional springerle board with incised and scoop-cut motifs.

The American colonial kitchen, or *keeping room*, was an absolute treasury of decorative carved woodwork. There were butter bowls and salt trays, Bible boxes and knife racks, pipe shelves and cutting boards, and of course the finely worked and beautifully carved food and cooking molds. From settlement to settlement, there were shortbread molds from Scotland, pastry rollers from England, breadboards from Sweden, cheese molds from Poland, and so on—all carved in the various mother countries' folk traditions. Perhaps best of all were the fancifully carved German springerle boards (FIG. 7-1).

In early Pennsylvania Dutch homes, every hausfrau needed a set of such molds. On high days and holidays, biscuit dough was rolled thin and pressed onto the carved hardwood boards, and then the whole thing was popped into the oven. When the biscuits were cooked, they were turned onto a plate and set out so that the little raised motifs and designs complemented the table arrangement. These uniquely beautiful boards were covered with delicate, primitively conceived, incised carvings of flower motifs, figures, and childlike interpretations of small birds and animals (FIG. 7-2).

As for woodworking techniques, of course some of the settlers were trained carvers and woodworkers, but in the main, American colonial springerle boards were made by people who possessed few woodworking skills. So where did they start? Well the answer is simple enough. As with other pioneers, they just rolled up their sleeves and improvised as they went along. With crosscut saw, drawknife, adze, gouge, and knife, they went for the nearest tree, cut it down, split it into boards and slabs, and then started working and carving while the wood was still green.

Some of the patterns and designs were copies of remembered traditional motifs, but mostly the carvers developed an honest, direct, empirical trial-and-error method of working. If the wood didn't split, warp, bleed, or smell, and if the motifs could be set-in with a few crisp knife and gouge strokes, and if the motifs on the molded biscuit stood up proud, then the improvised experimental approach was valid.

Materials

A 5-x-8 inch, 1-inch-thick slab of close-grained, knot-free hardwood—plum, apple, or sycamore
Modeling paste

Tools

A bench clamp or holdfast
A V-section gouge
A spoon-bit gouge or a shallow straight gouge
A sharp knife
Graded sandpapers
A metal straightedge
Pencils, work-out paper; tracing paper; other general workshop items

Fig. 7-2. Inspirational designs—various boards worked between c. 1700 and 1850.

DESIGN AND TECHNIQUE

In many ways, this project is ideally suited for beginners in that it uses a small piece of prepared timber, simple techniques, and a basic tool kit. Have a look at the working drawings (FIG. 7-3) and the step-by-step illustrations and see how the board has been designed, set out, and worked. See how the various motifs are set within a 2½-x-2½-inch grid, and note how the designs and patterns are incised and shallowly scoop-cut.

When you have studied all the working methods, patterns, and details, and when you appreciate all the tool and material implications of the project, then take your work-out paper, draw up a grid, and rough-out your own designs. Try not to slavishly copy every detail, but rather bring in your own ideas and whimsies. For example, perhaps you could personalize the project and include your family crest, your initials, dates of weddings or christenings, puns on surnames, or whatever. Sketch and plan until you come up with a good workable design.

When you have achieved a well-considered master pattern, then line-in the main profiles and take a tracing. You might also make a little prototype. That is to say, make a few trial cuts on a piece of scrap wood, just to see how the various motifs might be achieved. Finally, one you have made a prototype, press a small piece of warm modeling paste, such as Plasticine, into the cuts, take note of the resultant cast, and then modify the depth and width of the cuts accordingly (FIG. 7-4).

Setting Out the Wood and First Cuts

When you get your wood back to the workshop, give it a good looking over. Make absolutely sure that it is clear of bark, grain twists, end splits, stains, mold, and dead knots. This done, pencil-press transfer the traced design through to the working face of the wood.

Now clamp the wood to the bench with C-clamps or a holdfast, then take the knife and the straightedge and score in the six frames that indicate the cutting or break lines between the biscuits. Work each frame with a single, clean ⅛-inch-deep cut.

Next, take the V-tool, check that the wood is secure, and, using the initial knife-incised lines as a guide, trench out the frames (FIG. 7-5). Try to keep the V-cuts straight and crisp, and be careful that your tool doesn't dig too deeply into the grain or skid across the wood. Work with a considered, controlled action—guiding the tool with one hand, and pushing and maneuvering with the other. Continue until the six-frame grid is nicely set out, as illustrated. Note that the V-section trench cuts on the wooden board will, of course, become raised ridges on the biscuits.

Gouge and Knife Work

Once you have cut in the grid, have another good long look at the master design, then take a soft pencil to the wood and reestablish the various pattern and motif

Fig. 7-3. Working drawings—the grid scale is about 2 squares to 1 inch.

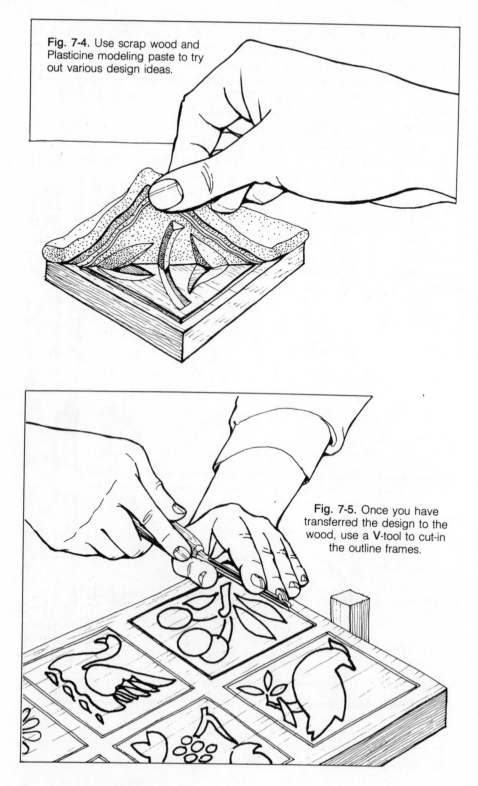

Fig. 7-4. Use scrap wood and Plasticine modeling paste to try out various design ideas.

Fig. 7-5. Once you have transferred the design to the wood, use a **V**-tool to cut-in the outline frames.

lines. If you are a beginner, it might also be a good idea at this stage to cross-hatch and label the areas that are going to be wasted and cut away. For example, you might shade in the cherries, the swan, and so on.

Now with the wood still securely clamped to the bench, take your chosen tool—either a spoon-bit gouge or a shallow-curved straight gouge—and start to scoop out the deepest part of each motif (FIG. 7-6). One frame at a time, scoop out the hollows of the cherries, the little hollows and dips that go to make up the rabbit, the berries, etc. Don't try to dig the tool straight down into the grain or gouge out great hunks of wood. Work the little concavities with a delicate scooping and paring action.

Cut across or at an angle to the grain wherever possible. Only remove small curls of wood, and try all the while to keep the carving crisp and controlled. If you feel at any time that your tool is cutting up rough, either approach the work from another angle or maybe give the cutting edge a couple of strokes on the stone or leather. Bear in mind as you work, that each and every motif needs to be smoothly, crisply, and directly carved—no undercuts, deep holes, torn grain, or rough surfaces.

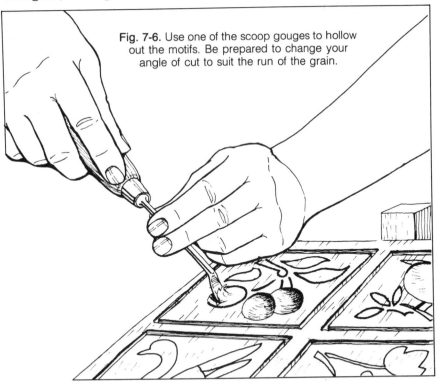

Fig. 7-6. Use one of the scoop gouges to hollow out the motifs. Be prepared to change your angle of cut to suit the run of the grain.

From time to time, warm up a piece of Plasticine and make a trial pressing. Note how the pressing lifts clear of the mold. See how the various incised lines and gouge cuts affect the cast, and then consider your progress. Could the hollows be deeper? Do the gouge-worked depressions produce nicely rounded, plump shapes? Be supercritical, and adjust your work accordingly.

FINISHING

When the main hollows of each motif have been scoop-cut and you are pleased with the overall design, then you need to cut in the final details and textures. First clear the work surface of all clutter. Now take a small V-section tool or a good sharp knife, and start to set-in all the little chip- and sliver-cut embellishments. That is, add the wing patterns, line in the various stalks and leaves, and generally carve all the other fine details that go to make up the total design (FIGS. 7-7 and 7-8).

Along the way, continue to take Plasticine impressions. See how all the chip cuts and nicks result in delicately raised and ridged details.

When you are pleased with your efforts, take the carving to a good, smooth finish; that is to say, make sure that the whole work is free from ragged edges and burrs. Finally wipe a little cooking oil into the grain, burnish the wood with a fluff-free cloth, and the job is done.

- If your are definitely going to hang your work on the wall, rather than use it for baking, then you can forget the cooking oil and use furniture wax.

- Children love playing with pastry, Plasticine, and clay. Maybe you could modify this project and make a toy?

- If you decide to make a board with initials, names, dates, and the like, remember that they need to be cut and worked in reverse, or mirror, image!

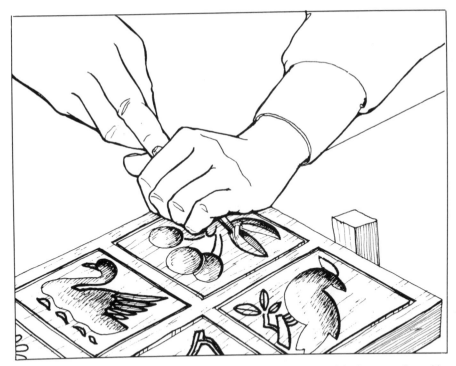

Fig. 7-7. When you come to carving the long leaf shapes, establish the centerline with a deep cut and then work at an angle into the cut to make a **V**-section form.

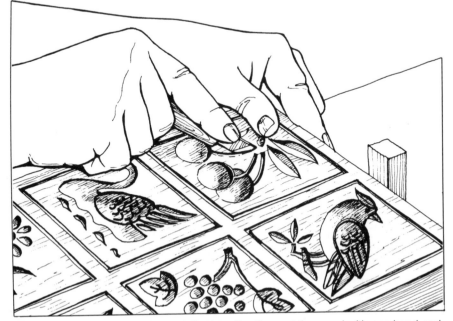

Fig. 7-8. Use a knife to work the delicate stalks. Support the wood with one hand and draw the blade toward you with the other.

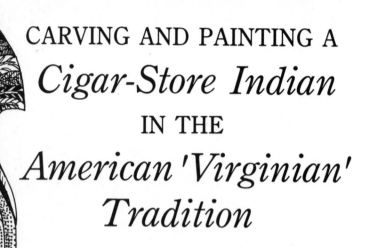

PROJECT 8

CARVING AND PAINTING A
Cigar-Store Indian
IN THE
American 'Virginian' Tradition

Fig. 8-1. An Indian cut from thick plank wood.
The forms are incised and semi-relief cut on
both sides of the wood to make a bas-relief.

86 WOODCARVING

Fig. 8-2. Inspirational designs

After a cigar-store Indian in
American Museum in Britain

Indian
7¼ feet high,
c.1870

Indian carved by
Julius Theodore Melchers,
72 inches high,
c.1865-67

After an Indian Maiden
seen at American
Museum in Britain

In England and America, the Red Indian has long been a figure of mystery and fascination (FIG. 8-1). For example, in England in the seventeenth-century, poets, artists, and romantics saw the Red Indian as a Virginian Prince, a Noble Savage, a dignified powerful figure, a figure dressed in a Greek-type kilt and flowing robes.

Although in England, the image of a Red Indian was linked with tobacco sales from a very early date, alongside other exotic characters like Turks, Blackamoors, Black Boys, and Egyptians, the idea of using an Indian as a tobacco store symbol didn't really catch on in America until well into the nineteenth century. At this time, the age of iron and steam was beginning to take over from that of wood and wind, and so it was that the craftsmen who had once carved the ship's figurehead and prow boards, now found new employment carving steam-ride horses, decorative formers for the cast iron foundries, shop signs, and of course cigar-store Indians. Better still, these self-same out-of-work figurehead carvers knew that in the shipyards there was a plentiful supply of straight-grained spar timber that was to be had for the asking. So it was that the towns and cities on the American Eastern Seaboard, the centers that had once supplied the materials and skills to create the figureheads, now became the centers of the sign and figure woodcarving industry.

Of course, just as the one-time ship carvers had used their primitive design skills to create grand, powerful, bold, thrusting, brightly painted, gold-embellished imagery, so now they used the same skills and techniques when they were working on the flamboyant shop signs and the cigar-store Indians. Could it be that the American nineteenth century cigar-store Indian carver was the initiator of that many-faced twentieth century monster: mass media and promotional advertising?

Materials

A large slab of knot-free lime wood, of a size to suit
Acrylic paints
Varnish

Tools

A good range of chisels and gouges, including: a V-tool
a shallow-curved straight gouge, a straight chisel
A mallet
A hand drill
At least two C-clamps
Shaping rasps
A bow and coping saw, a straight saw
A couple of sharp knives
Work-out paper, tracing paper, pencils
A measure
Sandpaper
Fine-point and broad brushes

Fig. 8-3. Working drawings—the grid scale is about 1 square to 2 inches. The design is not so much worked in the round, but rather incised and then the incisions used as stop cuts for long slanting cuts.

DESIGN AND TECHNIQUE

Have a look at our inspirational illustrations (FIG. 8-2) and working drawings (FIG. 8-3), and then visit a museum of folk art. Concentrate your studies on cigar-store Indians that were made between 1820 and about 1870. Also if possible, see ship's figureheads that were made at around the same period. When you view these, almost barbaric wood carvings, let your eyes and hands run over their form. Note the massive, direct lines of both the figureheads and the tobacco Indians, and see how the carvers have gone for the most dramatic, the most colorful, and perhaps the most obvious statement. Certainly to our eyes many or these figures look to be almost childlike in form and conception, and to have unrealistic proportions, fanciful costume details, and so on. Notice how the carvings are beautiful, powerful, and unique examples of the wood carver's art.

When you have studied as many cigar-store figures as possible, sit down with a work-out pad and make a series of elevation sketches. Draw the Indian from the front, the side, and so on. Take notes, make measurements, list the colors and, most importantly, try and take in the whole figure. See if you can analyze just what it is that makes cigar-store Indians so special.

Finally, have a look at our working drawings and see how our Indian is full size and carved in bas-relief. It is about 72 inches high, worked from 2- to 3-inch-thick slab or flat board, and carved on each side in low-curve flat relief.

Setting Out the Design and First Cuts

When you have studied as many cigar-store Indians as possible, meaning everything from small countertop figures through to full size and larger-than-life figures, then take note of all your museum sketches and draw up a full-size master design. Also make tracings of both side elevations. This done, check your wood over for faults, and reject materials that look to be split, sappy, knotty, or in any way less than perfect.

Now, take one or other of the traced side views, and pencil-press transfer the traced lines through to one face of your plank. Once you have transferred the design, pencil over the main lines, block in the areas that need to be fretted out, and generally label and organize the wood. After you have clearly established the profile of the Indian on one side of the wood, secure the slab with a C-clamp so that some part of it hangs over the edge of the workbench. With the drill, straight saw, and bow saw, rough-out the basic Indian form.

Turn the wood over so that the pencil lines on the first side are face down, then pencil-press transfer the lines of the other profile—that is, the second side—through to the other side of the wood (FIG. 8-4). This done, take a V-section tool and go over the pencil lines on both sides of the wood, cutting clean V-section trenches (FIG. 8-5).

Setting In and Wasting

Once you have established and V-trenched all the lines of the design, then sit back and take another long look at the project picture and the working drawings.

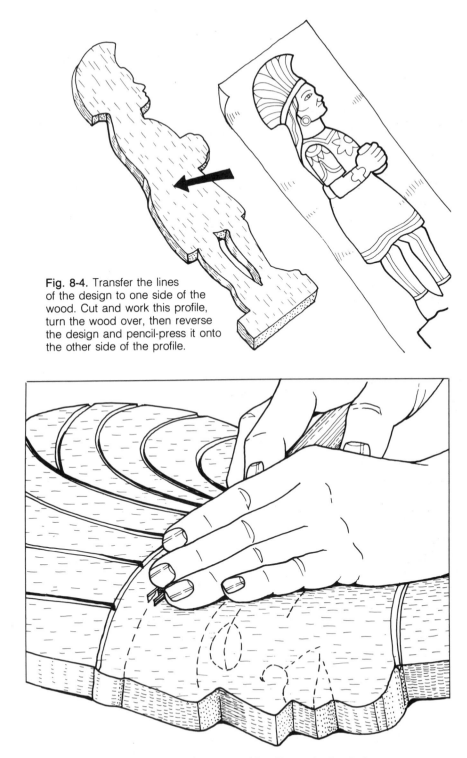

Fig. 8-4. Transfer the lines of the design to one side of the wood. Cut and work this profile, turn the wood over, then reverse the design and pencil-press it onto the other side of the profile.

Fig. 8-5. On one side at a time, use a **V**-tool to cut-in the design.

See how, although the various parts of the figure look to be cut-in to some considerable depth, in fact the carving technique relates more to shallow rounded relief than to realistic carving in-the-round. The whole carving is made up of shallow "valleys" and rounded "hills"; there are no undercuts. For example, although the arm appears to stand out from the rest of the form, this is more an illusion that a reality. The illusion is created by sharply cutting, lowering, and rounding the wood immediately around the arm (FIG. 8-6). And so it is with the chin, the belt, around the hand, at the top of the leg, and so on.

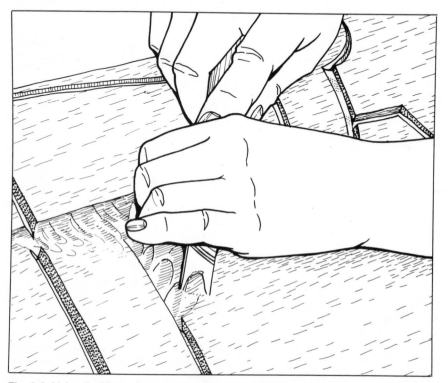

Fig. 8-6. Using the V-trenches as stop cuts, work and shape the motifs to give an illusion of roundness.

Once you appreciate just how these areas need to be carved, then work around the main forms with angled, sloping cuts. For example, when you want to carve the arm, take a shallow-curve gouge and go around the arm cutting in toward the V-trench. Work right around the form; that is, from just below the shoulder, down the front of the arm, around the clenched fist, around the tobacco leaves, up the back of the arm, and into the armpit. As you work, you will find that the V-cut trench acts as a stop cut, and the wood around the arm will come away as wedge-shaped chips or slices.

When you have worked once around the arm, then rework the original V-cut and repeat the procedure. When the arm looks to be standing out from the slab, then continue to work the other main forms in like manner.

Modeling the Forms

When you have angled the wood immediately around each of the main forms, then stand back and see how the figure begins to look slightly three-dimensional. Of course, you can't continue to angle and lower the wood and go for modeled realism, because after all the plank of wood is only 2 to 3 inches thick. All you can do is to aim for relief-worked stylization.

When you have established the primary forms, take a knife or gouge and gently cut away and round-off all the sharp corners and edges of the high-relief areas (FIG. 8-7). Feel your way around the elements that go to make up the figure—the face, the shoulders, the arm, the hands and so on. Continue until the various design elements gradually appear to be layered one on top of another. Finally, with rasp and gouge, round-off the edges of the slab and run the figure details round the thickness of the wood.

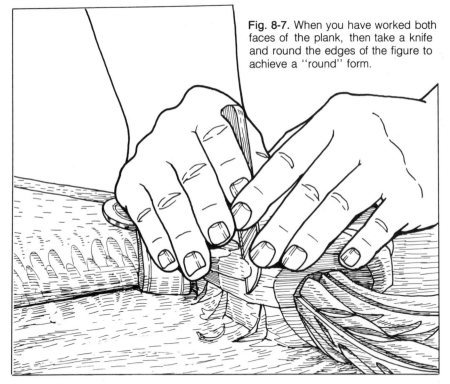

Fig. 8-7. When you have worked both faces of the plank, then take a knife and round the edges of the figure to achieve a "round" form.

The Details and Patterns

Once you have set-in, lowered, and rounded the main forms, you can begin to carve and line-in the patterns and details. Just as you carved and cut into the stop cuts that set out the main forms, so you can, in miniature, repeat the procedure with the pattern details on the costume—the stripes that go up the legs and around the hem of the kilt, the feathers, and all the other patterns and motifs.

After you have worked and carved all the details and patterns, and are reasonably pleased with the overall feel of the figure, then give the whole carving a quick tooled finish. Tidy up an edge here, cut and sharpen a pattern detail there, and generally go over the whole figure, making sure that all the details are crisply worked and pulled together. This done, brush out all the angles and corners, and make sure that the project is free from dust and shavings.

PAINTING

When you consider the carving finished, then clear away the clutter and set out the acrylic paints and your selection of brushes. Start by establishing the main colors. You will need a red-bronze color for the face, arms, and hands; a dark muted green color for the robe and the kilt; buff yellow for the leggings and some of the feathers; gold for the earrings, the costume patterns, the trim, the sash, the wrist jewelry, and the decorative band around the bottom of the kilt hem.

Lay on the large areas of ground color first, and gradually work, as it were, upward toward a finish (FIG. 8-8). Wait for the ground colors to dry before you build up successive color layers. Don't try for realism by mixing subtle colors; just lay the paints on as flat, thin washes.

Finally, when the paint is dry, give the whole figure a couple of coats of varnish, and the job is done.

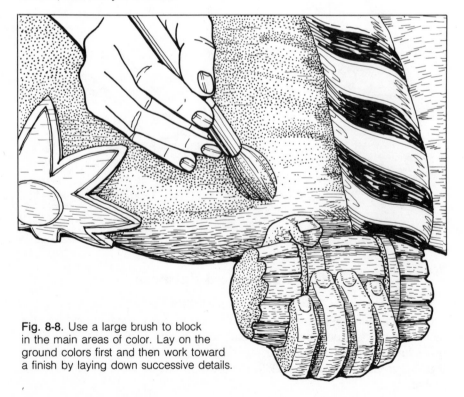

Fig. 8-8. Use a large brush to block in the main areas of color. Lay on the ground colors first and then work toward a finish by laying down successive details.

- If you want to work and carve a fully rounded figure, look to one of the other projects for technique guidance.

- When you are choosing wood, go for easy-to-carve, smooth-grained varieties like lime and sycamore.

- The finished Indian can either be hung like a screen, mounted on a beam of timber, or mounted on a box-built plinth.

PROJECT 9

PAINTING A
Hope Chest
IN THE
18th Century American Tradition

Fig. 9-1. A traditional and characteristic chest with three arched architectural panels and painted flower motifs.

Fig. 9-2. Inspirational designs—designs from Pennsylvanian chests made and painted between c. 1720 and 1850. Note the tulips, the hex circles, the arched forms, and the dot-and-dash edge details.

In Pennsylvania in the eighteenth century, it was the custom for maidens, when they reached marriagable age or on their betrothal, to be given large, decorative, brilliantly painted chests (FIG. 9-1). Known variously as *hope, dower,* or *dowery chests,* these lavish, exuberant, wonderfully and elaborately decorated boxes were not just pieces of furniture, as was a cupboard or a set of chairs. They were symbolic expressions of life, hope, and family.

Ornamented with names, dates, and all manner of motifs and symbols, the American dower chest tradition has its roots in Old-World folk beliefs and customs. The Pennsylvania Dutch, and immigrants from Holland, Sweden, Switzerland, and Poland all had traditions of making, decorating, and giving such chests. So it is that hope chests aren't the product of any single Old-World craft or custom, but rather they are the coming together of many customs. This fact is borne out by the structure, decoration, imagery, and design of such pieces. For example, the characteristic three-panel layout, whether it be achieved simply by painting or by facade moldings, relates to much earlier European chests that needed technically to be jointed, built, and carved.

The actual decorative motifs—the hearts, unicorns, tulips, the three-petal flowers, the fanciful birds, the hex stars, and even the choice of colors—are all ancient and symbolic (FIG. 9-2). For example, in medieval times unicorns were thought of as the guardians of virginal purity. In pre-Christian times, yellow was considered to be a magic color and sacred to the god Donar. Hex motifs have to do with the old German belief that witches on horseback rode through the night and sought to do us harm, (nightmares). As to who painted American hope boxes, just as house interiors were painted variously by itinerants, the man of the house, or local craftsmen, so it was with the hope chests.

Of course, from county to county and period to period, the form and style of chest decoration changed, but American folk hope chests can be characterized by their three-panel layout; the rich, primitive floral designs, such as tulips, vines, and stylized flowers; the balusters and borders all filled with free pattern; and the use of bold colors, such as yellow, reds, greens, and blues.

Materials

An item to be decorated, such as a chest or a wooden panel
Acrylic paints

Tools

A sketchbook, a drawing board
Pencils
A pair of compasses
A ruler
A straightedge
Sandpaper
Tracing paper
Masking tape
A selection of broad and fine-point brushes
Usual workshop items, like paint dishes, cloths, and newspapers

DESIGN AND TECHNIQUE

Start by having a look at our inspirational designs (FIG. 9-2), working drawings (FIG. 9-3), and details. Although the outer panel designs of our project are in themselves asymmetrical—that is to say, the layout of the flowers is off-center and there is a little bird on one side of the main stem—when the design is mirror-image reversed and used as two flanking panels, then the total chest design becomes symmetrical. Take note of all the inspirational motifs and details, and see how the dower chest painters favored strong, bold forms and beautiful dot-and-dash zigzag borders.

Search out your item to be decorated—a tabletop, an old chest, the front of a cupboard or whatever. Consider just how you want your piece to be decorated. For example, are you going to copy the project in every detail? Are you going to modify the design and only decorate a single panel? Are you going to mix your own oil or milk paints, rather than use acrylics? Are you going to actually make and decorate a paneled chest, including name and date? You need to consider all these points carefully before you set out.

When you have tackled all these points in turn and have made a decision as to design, color, and layout, then take a trip to the nearest American folk museum. Look at chests dated 1780-1810.

Finally, in the light of your researches, make a series of design sketches and draw up your own master design. That is to say, draw up the panels to size, settle on colors (FIG. 9-4), decide on the order of work, organize your working area, make sure that you have a good selection of brushes, and generally tidy up all the loose ends.

Preparing the Ground and Transferring the Design

When you have drawn up your master design and are pleased with the way it relates to the item to be decorated, then make a good tracing. Now take the item—for example, an old chest—and make sure that it is clean and well prepared. To this end, remove all the old paint and varnish, make sure all nail heads are punched well below the surface of the wood, and fill splits and knots. Remove, repair, or replace damaged or broken hinges and catches, and generally bring the item to good order. When the chest has been rubbed down with the graded sandpapers, remove all the waste with a stiff brush, and wipe it down with a damp cloth (FIG. 9-5).

Now decide on the ground color. We chose a good bright yellow ochre. Mix enough to cover, and then lay on a single, well-brushed coat. Don't worry too much if the grain of the wood shows through the paint because in many ways this is to the good. Just try to paint out repairs, stains, and knots.

When the ground paint is dry, give the work a swift rubbing down with a fine-grade sandpaper, and start to transfer and set out the design. If you are modifying the project and working on a flat-faced six-board chest, rather than a framed chest with inset panels, then draw out the three arched panels with a ruler, straightedge, square, and a compass, and number them from left to right 1, 2, and 3. Now tape the traced design carefully in place on panel 1, and

Fig. 9-3. Working drawings—scale to suit.

Fig. 9-4. Color grid—colors to suit. It is best to go for bold contrasts.

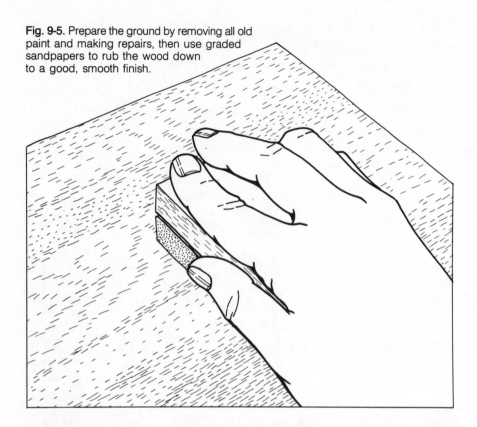

Fig. 9-5. Prepare the ground by removing all old paint and making repairs, then use graded sandpapers to rub the wood down to a good, smooth finish.

pencil-press transfer the lines of the tracing through to the surface that is to be decorated (FIG. 9-6). (NOTE: if you are working on a piece of furniture that has inset panels, then you will need to cut the tracing paper so that it fits inside the panel.) This done, carefully remove and reverse the tracing, tape it in place on panel 3, and then pencil-press transfer as already described.

Working in this way, you can be sure that the total design is symmetrical. NOTE: in this project it is intended that the central panel should contain names, dates, and the like.

When you have checked that all is correct, take a hard pencil and go over the transferred lines making sure that they are well established. When the design has been set out, have a look at your working drawings and color notes, then mix the rest of your ground colors accordingly. Finally, lay on the other main background colors, for example the band of color that goes around each of the three arched panels. If you desire, you might also, while the paint is still wet, experiment with one or other of the traditional texturing effects. You could dab the paint with a screw of newspaper, or smoke the paint with a candle, or comb a design with a cardboard strip. See the *Workshop Data* section and study American hope chests in museum collections. Note how the decorators worked such dramatic effects as rippled grain and *paw print*.

Generally bring the ground colors and the transferred lines to good order in readiness for the decorative painting.

Fig. 9-6. When the ground color is dry, tape the tracing into position and then pencil-press the lines of the traced design through to the chest.

Black-line Striping and Blocking in the Colors

When the ground colors are dry, then take your finest long-haired brush—it is best really to use a striping brush. Make sure that the black paint is well mixed, then set to painting in the lines of the design (FIG. 9-7). Dip the full length of the brush hairs in the paint, make a swift trial stroke on a scrap of card, and then go to work. Draw the brush toward you along the guidelines, all the while aiming for lines that are smooth, even, and confident.

When the design has been striped in, leave it until the paint is dry. While you are waiting for the paint to dry—and this might take anything from a couple of hours to a couple of days, depending on whether or not you are using fast-drying acrylics or slow-drying japan paint—refresh your eye by having a look at your sketch notes, inspirational drawings, and working designs.

Now mix your colors to a good consistency and then start blocking in the main design windows—the vase, the flower stems, the tulip petals, and so on (FIG. 9-8). Continue until you consider the design finished, then generally tidy up details and repair errors—adjust black lines, pick out dot-and-dash embellishments with a fine brush, and line in the details of the birds.

Fig. 9-7. Use a long-haired brush and black paint to line-in the design. See how the little finger might be extended to steady your stroke.

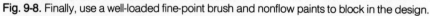

Fig. 9-8. Finally, use a well-loaded fine-point brush and nonflow paints to block in the design.

Finally, when the blocks of color are dry, swiftly rub the box down with the finest of sandpapers and lay on a couple of coats of varnish. NOTE: never varnish on a warm, rainy day. Be sure to work in an area that is dust free, and always let the first coat of varnish dry thoroughly before you rub down and revarnish.

- Traditionally, some painters blocked in the colors, varnished, and then black-line striped. Make a trial run and then modify the project to suit your needs and skills.

- See the *Workshop Data* section for traditional paint and technique variations.

CARVING AND PAINTING A
Wild Fowl Decoy
IN THE
American Gunner
Tradition

Fig. 10-1. A traditional decoy with
semi-stylized feather patterning.

Fig. 10-2. Inspirational designs—a selection of nineteenth century American wild fowl decoys.

As to when and where the first Red Indians started to make wild fowl decoys, who can say? Enough to know that when the Colonial American trappers saw the stick-and-mud decoys being used by the Indians, they took up the idea and developed it using Western wood-carving methods and techniques (FIG. 10-1).

The word *decoy,* in the context of this project, has several possible roots, but it probably came from the Dutch words *kooj, de kooi,* or *koye,* meaning to lure, entice, or snare.

The point of using decoys was straightforward enough. Woodcarved and painted wild fowl were anchored in a likely position around a lake edge. Passing flocks of wild fowl were attracted by the look-alikes, so they settled on the water, providing easy targets for the hunters and gunners. From our present, conservative standpoint, mass wild-fowl ambushes—that is to say commercial shoots on a huge scale where hundreds of birds are killed in a day—look to be altogether unpleasant. However, from a hungry settler's point of view, it was a very efficient way of hunting! In fact, it was so efficient that by 1920 or thereabouts, Congress banned large-scale commercial *gunner* shooting on the grounds that the practice was wiping out whole species of wild fowl.

The decoys were traditionally made by the hunters themselves. With axe, knife, and found wood, the bodies were worked to a rough approximation; the heads were whittled to fit; the two were pegged, jointed, or spiked together; then finally the whole form was swiftly painted. As to design, the decoy makers weren't concerned with "perfect in every feather" details; they were only after the overall, seen-from-a-distance image and effect (FIG. 10-2).

Of course, with the passing of the years, wild-fowl decoys have become precious collectibles. The simple wild-fowl forms and look-alikes are now considered prime examples of primitive, sculptural American folk art.

Materials

About 4 feet of rough-sawn 9-x-2¼-inch easily worked wood, such as smooth-grained pine, cedar, or, best of all, lime
A quantity of PVA adhesive
A selection of acrylic paints, colors to suit.

Tools

A sketch pad and pencil
Tracing paper
A mallet
A mortise chisel
A straight saw
A bow saw or a band saw
A large crooked knife
A straight clasp knife
A couple of large C-clamps
A bench and vise
A selection of long-haired broad and fine-pointed brushes

DESIGN AND TECHNIQUE

Before you put tools to wood, stop and consider just how you want your decoy to be worked. For example, do you want to make a very detailed duck study? Will you be using a band saw? Would you prefer to use a set of gouges, rather than a crooked knife? Are you going to spike the head to the body? Decisions like these need careful consideration before you start.

Also, before you rush out and buy your wood, try to gather as much background data as possible. Visit art centers, craft shows, and museums of American folk art. Note on your travels how variously decoys are/were built and put together. See how the forms are painted. If possible, handle old decoys, feel out their weight, structure, and size, and try to evaluate their design.

This done, sit back with a sketch pad and gridded paper and make a series of well worked up drawings. Show all views, elevations, profiles, colors, and fixings. If you are a beginner, you might also take a lump of clay or modeling paste and make a maquette or working model.

As you are considering the design, don't be afraid to reassess the forms in terms of your own likes and dislikes. Be ready to adjust the sculptural forms to suit your own requirements.

Finally, make a series of full-size working drawings—drawings complete with measurements and color details (FIGS. 10-3 and 10-4). NOTE: you might also at this stage start a collection of wild-fowl magazine clips, photographs, and studies.

Setting Out the Wood

Pin your studies up around your working area. Decide what size you want your decoy to be, and then arrange your tools so that they are comfortably at hand. Now set your wood out on the workbench and check it over to make sure that it is relatively free from dead knots, awkward grain twists, stains, and splits.

Take your working drawing, make a good tracing, then pencil-press transfer the traced lines through to the working face of the wood. Make sure that you have the grain running from head to tail, and from the tip of the beak to the back of the head crest. When you have transferred the tracing, then go over the transferred lines with a soft pencil, and label the various drawn profiles and the waste.

First Cuts, Gluing, and Clamping

Start by swiftly cutting out the three forms—that is, the two bodies and the head. Remove all the waste. Don't try to achieve anything like a finished form; just settle for knocking off all the corners and getting as close as you can to the drawn lines.

Now take the best of the two body slabs—that is, the one with the best grain—have a look at the working drawing just to see how the head slots into a body mortise, and then mark out the wood accordingly (FIG. 10-5.) Check that all is correct. Make sure the marked out body relates to the head, then, with the mallet and the straight chisel, chop out the mortise. Remove the waste with

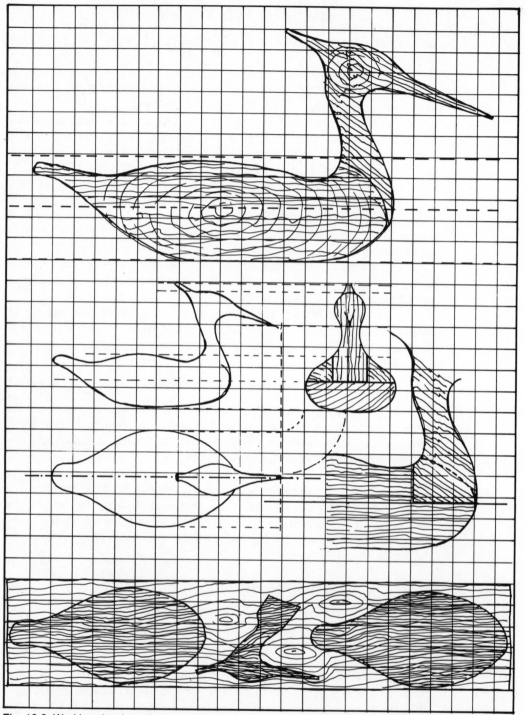

Fig. 10-3. Working drawing—the top grid scale is about 1 square to 1 inch; the bottom grid scale is about 1 square to 2 inches. Note the various profiles, views, and construction details. See also how you can cut the wood to use the grain to best advantage.

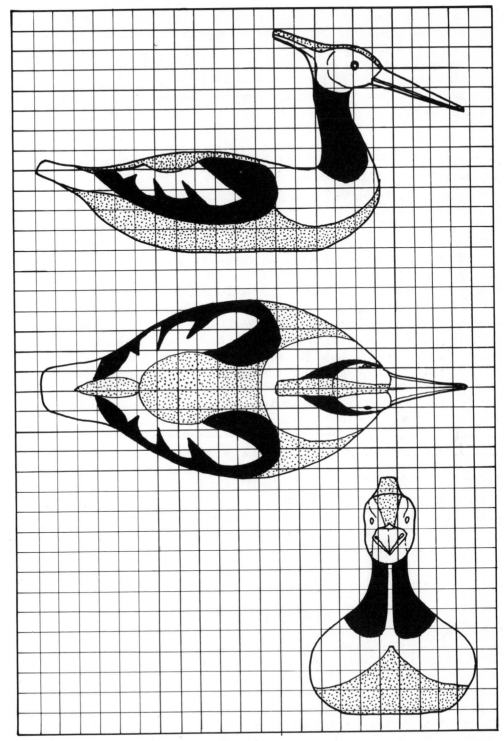

Fig. 10-4. Painting grid—side, plan, and front views.

care and aim for a push-tight fit. When this has been done, have a trial fitting and, if necessary, adjust the mortise and/or the base of the neck so that the head sits at a suitable angle.

Having made sure that the two body pieces and the head come together and make a good fit, smear PVA adhesive on the underside of the top body slab, all around the base of the neck, and in the body mortise. Then bring the three pieces of wood together and clamp up.

Removing the Main Areas of Waste and Working the Body

When the glue is dry, remove the clamps, set the duck out on the work surface, and then have a good, long look at our inspirational illustrations (FIG. 10-2) and your working drawings. Note how, on the side view, the duck angles in from tail to base, and from breast to base. Mark out your wood with a soft pencil, establish in your own mind just how much waste needs to be removed, then take the straight saw and work the wood accordingly. Remove a large wedge from the underside of the tail, and from the underside of the breast (FIG. 10-6).

This done, place the duck so that you can see him head on, have another look at the working drawings, and then mark off the areas of waste each side of the head crest and either side of the face and the beak. Again, take the straight saw and swiftly remove the waste. You should now have an angular ducklike form.

Now, working with a large knife—it is best to use a Northwest Canadian Indian crooked knife—begin to carve and work the body. Keeping one eye on your pinned-up inspirational drawings and the other eye on the wood, work the form from center to end. Aim, as near as possible, to cut at an angle to the grain. Don't try to remove great chunks of wood or do a rush job, but rather only remove little wisps and scalloped curls of wood (FIG. 10-7).

Continue until the duck body becomes sharp ended and begins to take on ducklike characteristics. The whole form should have a very low center of gravity, and the main body bulge should be well below the waterline. Continue cutting, taking caliper readings, referring to the working drawings, and all the while removing the wood little by little until you gradually get closer and closer to the required duck form.

The Head

Go back to your various museum studies and working drawings, and see how the beak and head crest relate to the bird's neck, breast, and body. Now support the duck in your lap or on the work surface and set to with the crooked knife. Work with care and caution. Again, don't try to rush; just work at a gentle, even, relaxed pace. If you are using a crooked knife, never work with great slashing, uncontrolled strokes. Always use your thumb as a pivotal lever; that is to say, push the handle of the knife with your thumb, and in so doing hook the blade toward you with a scooping action. Let the blade slice off delicate, dappled, and scooped curls.

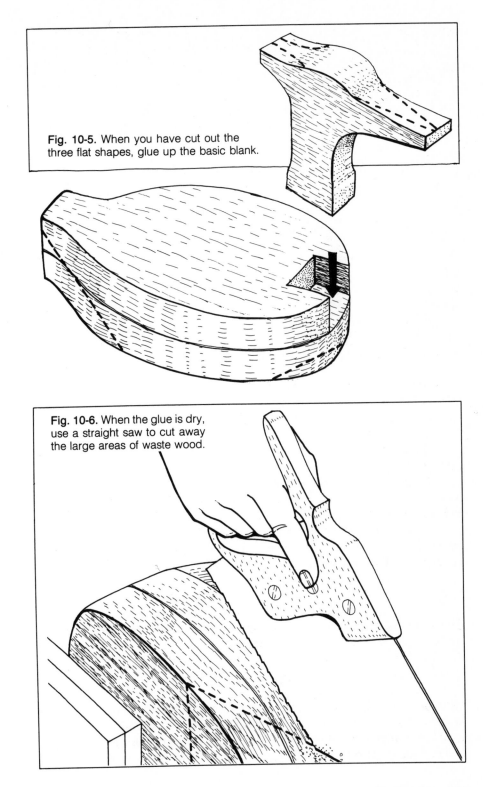

Fig. 10-5. When you have cut out the three flat shapes, glue up the basic blank.

Fig. 10-6. When the glue is dry, use a straight saw to cut away the large areas of waste wood.

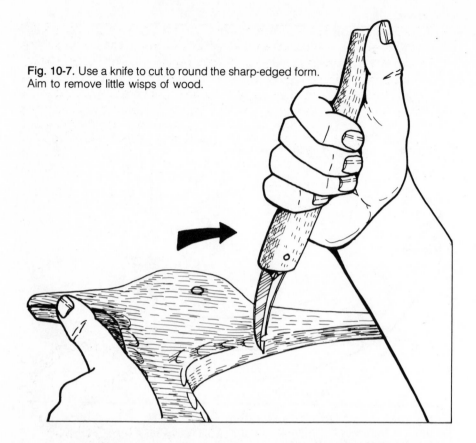

Fig. 10-7. Use a knife to cut to round the sharp-edged form. Aim to remove little wisps of wood.

As you get closer to the required head form, then ease off with the strength of the knife cuts and only remove the most minute wisps of wood. If, as you are working you have doubts as to just how a particular form or curve should be cut, then take a scrap of modeling paste and maybe a scrap of wood, and have few tryouts.

Of course as you are working, always watch the run of the grain, and be ready to adjust the direction of your cuts accordingly. Be extra careful when you come to the fragile short-grain areas on and around the neck.

Continue carving, taking caliper readings, standing back from the work and being supercritical, and then continuing to carve until the work is finished.

NOTE: although in this project we have chosen to take the decoy to a dappled and tooled finished, you might prefer to use graded sandpapers and go for a completely smooth finish. The choice is yours.

PAINTING AND FINISHING

When you have achieved a good form—and this might take anything from a couple of days to a couple of months, depending upon how much work you put in— then put all your tools away and clear the work surface of all dust and clutter. Set out your acrylic paints and wipe the decoy over with a damp cloth.

Use a soft brush to lay on a very thin white base coat. While this ground coat is drying, take a scrap of wood—a scrap that has already been painted white—and try out various painting techniques. You can use dappling, smudging, dry-brush printing, fluid-line painting, working with thick flat colors, working with thin color washes, experimenting with masses of swirling pattern, and so on.

When you have experimented with the various brushes and methods of applying the paint, then be bold and paint the decoy to suit. Don't, in the first instance, try for realistic feathers and features. It is much better to go for large areas of color (FIG. 10-8). Finally, when you consider your decoy to be well painted, then lay on a couple of coats of matte varnish, and the job is done.

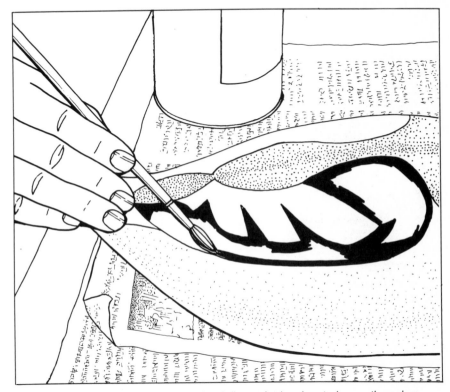

Fig. 10-8. Use acrylic paints and soft fine-point brushes to lay on the colors.

- You can, if you so wish, work this project with a selection of gouges and a drawknife. See other projects.

- Acrylic paints dry very quickly. Wash your brushes as soon as you are finished with them.

(. . . continued)

- If possible, paint your decoy away from the dusty woodworking area, but still wipe the wood over with a damp cloth before you start painting.

- Crooked or hooked knives need to be handled with great care. Use them with a thumb-controlled hooking action. In the wrong hands such a knife can be very dangerous—be warned.

PROJECT 11

WORKING A
Chip-Carved Serving Board
IN THE
Medieval English Tradition

Fig. 11-1. A serving board with traditional circle-based hex-flower and radius chip-cut design.

Of all the decorative wood-carving techniques, chip carving is at one and the same time perhaps the oldest, the most attractive, the easiest to do and the most widely used (FIG. 11-1). In essence, it is a beautifully direct and simple process in which the surface to be decorated is set out and gridded geometrically, and then worked with a systematic series of regular triangular cuts or pockets.

By repeating a number of carefully considered and well-organized vertical and sloping cuts, and by varying the depth, profile, and overall arrangement of the cuts, it is possible to decorate all manner of smooth and undulating surfaces with the most beautiful and attractive designs, motifs, and patterns. With a few basic tools—a couple of knives, sometimes a straight chisel and a shallow curve gouge, and a set of dividers—the carver sets out triangulated geometrical patterns and then works the triangular pockets of wood with direct stab-and-slice cuts.

Beautiful, easy to do, and uncomplicated—chip carving is all of these, but better still, it is by its very nature delightfully flexible in that it can be modified and adjusted to suit the job in hand. For example, a chip-carved design can be extended and used as a total cover pattern or texture, or it can be restricted and contained, as in this project, and used as a single one-off circle or roundel motif.

English medieval chip-carved roundels are characterized by having sharp-edged triangles and petal-lozenge or boat-shaped cuts, all being set within a compass-drawn hex. That is to say, a circle is set out with a compass or dividers and then stepped off and subdivided to form a hexagon. A successful chip-carved design of this character doesn't need to be deeply worked or in any way undercut, but rather it needs to be very carefully measured and set out, and then crisply and rhythmically worked.

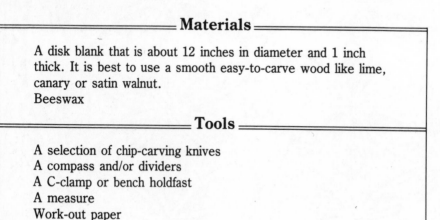

Materials

A disk blank that is about 12 inches in diameter and 1 inch thick. It is best to use a smooth easy-to-carve wood like lime, canary or satin walnut.
Beeswax

Tools

A selection of chip-carving knives
A compass and/or dividers
A C-clamp or bench holdfast
A measure
Work-out paper
A soft brush

Fig. 11-2. Inspirational designs—various circle-based chip-carved designs.

Fig. 11-3. Working drawings—the grid scale is about 2 squares to 1 inch. Note how the whole pattern has been compass-drawn.

DESIGN AND TECHNIQUE

Have a good, long look at our inspirational designs (FIG. 11-2) and working drawings (FIG. 11-3), and see how the grid needs to be carefully considered and set-in. See how the roundel design is circle based, meaning that it fits within a circle. It is also made up from a number of circles and arcs. See also how the main design and all the small areas within the main design relate to hex flowers and radius-drawn petals.

Before you start the project, take a sheet of work-out paper and a compass, and make a series of exploratory drawings and designs. If you are a beginner, don't be put off by what looks at first sight to be a really tricky project. Play around with a compass and experiment until you are able to confidently draw out the design. Of course, if on consideration, you feel that the design is altogether too complicated or too simple, then there is no reason at all why you shouldn't adjust and modify it to suit your own needs and skill level.

Also if you are a beginner, it would be a good idea at this stage to take a compass, a scrap of wood, and a knife, and to have a few trial cuts. See how by making two stop cuts and then by running the knife across and down into the stop cuts it is possible to work a beautiful triangular pocket. Again, play around with the knife and try various cuts until you feel confident.

Finally, visit a museum and get to see as many examples of chip carving as possible. Have a look at eighteenth and nineteenth century folk chip carvings as worked by peasants in Switzerland and central Europe, but center your research on the larger, bolder carvings, as worked on English medieval chests and coffers.

Setting Out the Roundel

When you are happy with your practice cuts and when you have chosen a suitable design or modified ours, then take your blank and check it over for faults. If your blank looks to be in any way less than perfect—meaning if the wood is stained, split, warped, or if there are any awkward or suspect knots—then reject it. It is most important with a project of this character that the wood be as near flawless as possible.

Now take the dividers, knife, and measure, and set out the design (FIG. 11-4). Don't rush at it or try in the first instance to score the lines of the design too deeply; just aim to get the design positioned correctly. When you have achieved what you consider is a good design, then go over the guidelines with the dividers and cut-in to a depth of about $\frac{1}{16}$ inch (FIG. 11-5).

When you have set out all the petals and arcs in this manner, then take a knife, and set out all the little diamonds at the petal-lozenge centers. Finally, take the knife to the outer border and establish the beautiful little zigzag pattern.

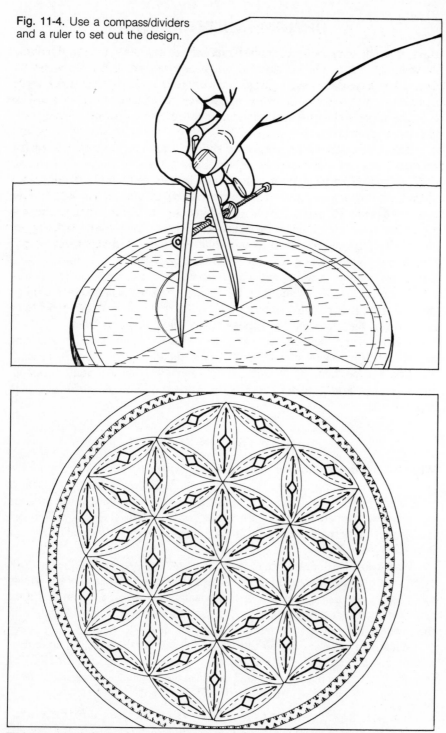

Fig. 11-4. Use a compass/dividers and a ruler to set out the design.

Fig. 11-5. The thick lines indicate deep downward cuts. The thin lines indicate shallow incised cuts. The dotted lines indicate areas to be sliced at an angle.

Setting in the First Cuts

When all the lines of the design have been set out with dividers and the point of a knife, and when you are sure that all is correct, then secure the wood on the bench with the C-clamp or holdfast. Before you go any further, stop a moment and have another look at your working drawings. See how the central motif is built up from a very basic form: the petal-lozenge, or boat shape. Focus your attention on a single lozenge and see how, although it is complicated by having long curved sides and a diamond-shaped central relief area, it is really no more than four chip cuts that are worked back to back.

Take your knife to a single lozenge, as marked out on your wood, and make a firm downward cut from the point of the diamond through to the point of the lozenge (FIG. 11-6). This done, repeat the cut to set-in the other half of the lozenge, then cut-in all four sides of the diamond. Repeat for all the petal lozenges that go to make up the total motif. That is to say, set-in each petal-lozenge shape with six cuts, straight down into the wood as illustrated.

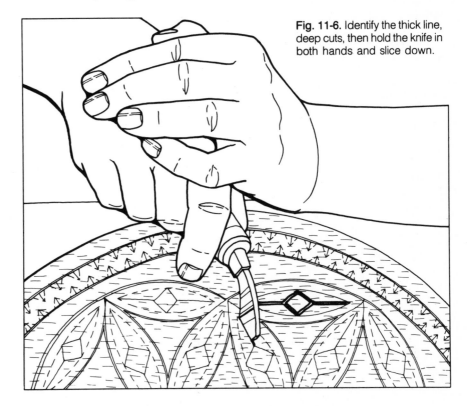

Fig. 11-6. Identify the thick line, deep cuts, then hold the knife in both hands and slice down.

Working the Triangular Chip Cuts

All the petal-lozenge forms should now be set in with the six stab or stop cuts. Now, making sure that the wood is secure, take the knife of your choice, select one or other of the lozenge forms, and begin. Hold the knife at a low angle to the working surface of the wood, support it with both hands, and then slide it around the curved side of the lozenge and into the body of the wood (FIG. 11-7). Slide the point of the knife in as far as the stop cuts, then twist the blade slightly and lift out a little triangular sliver. Depending on your choice of wood, your knife, and your strength, you might need to work each little triangular nick several times, and, as it were, remove the wood in successive layers.

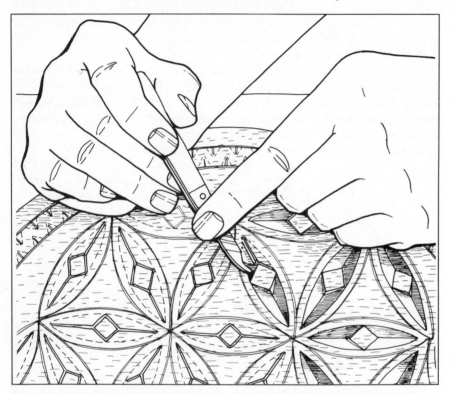

Fig. 11-7. After you have made the deep cuts, hold the knife at an angle and slide it around in a curve to remove long slivers of wood.

Continue until the triangular pocket is clean cut, at the right depth, and crisply worked. Do this with all four quarters that go to make up the lozenge, then work all the other lozenges in like manner.

If, as you are working, the wood starts to cut up rough, then stop and spend time resharpening the knife. Working with a blunt knife is not only difficult and frustrating, but it is also dangerous. Another word of caution: with a work of this character, mistakes and overcuts are very difficult to conceal or correct. This being so, always look twice and cut once. If you have any doubts as to the order of work or the direction of a cut or whatever, then go back to your scrap of wood, or a piece of modeling paste and sort the problems out by trial and error before you continue.

Working the Zigzag Border

When you have worked the main motif, then you can consider carving the zigzag border. Have a look at the working drawings and see how, as with the main design, the little zigzags are no more than triangular pockets. See also how each triangle needs to be set-in with two stab or stop cuts: one at the base, and one from point to base.

Now, one pocket at a time, work around the zigzag border, setting in each triangle with the two stop cuts. This done, select one pocket, hold the knife at an angle to the working face of the roundel, and then slide it into the triangle from side to center. Again, don't try to remove the waste in one great thrust. It is much better to work deeper and deeper with say two or three successive cuts. Each triangle needs to be worked with two stop cuts and half a dozen or so slanting cuts.

Continue, systematically working the little ribbon of pockets that go to make up the total zigzag border design. When all the pockets have been cut, spend time bringing the knife to a razor-sharp edge, then go over the whole project swiftly, cleaning out the various cuts, angles, valleys, and ridges (FIG. 11-8). Aim to leave the wood looking sharp edged, crisp, and tool burnished.

Fig. 11-8. Finally use the knife point to clean out all the small corners and crannies.

FINISHING

When you consider the carving to be more or less complete, stand back and give it a really critical inspection. Now, bearing in mind that a work of this character needs to be clean and crisp, run your eyes and your fingertips over the chip cuts and search out imperfections and faults. If necessary, take your finest, sharpest scalpel and deepen angles, sharpen ridges, and so on.

When you consider the work finished, brush out all the pockets with a soft brush, and then remove all the bench waste and clutter. Finally, dust down the wood, wipe it over with beeswax, let it stand for 24 hours or so, and then use a brush to burnish it to a warm-shine finish.

- If you want to darken your wood slightly prior to beeswaxing, use an oil mixture—3 parts linseed oil to 1 part turpentine.

- If you are using a compass, rather than a set of dividers, set the lines of the design in with a small V-tool. Don't cut too deeply; just work a very delicate incised line.

- Chip carvings need to be totally considered at the setting out stage. Even with a basic design of this type, it is most important that all the lines be clean, well established, and accurate.

- The triangular pockets need to be about ⅛ to ¼ inch deep, no deeper.

- When you have finished, don't be tempted to rub the wood down with sandpaper. In this context, sanding is not recommended. Don't worry about trying to remove guidelines. They are an attractive part of the total design.

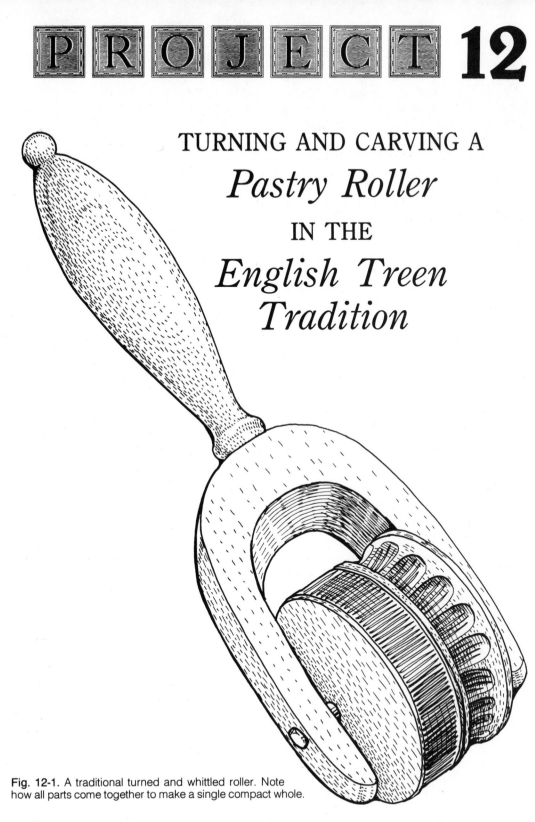

PROJECT 12

TURNING AND CARVING A
Pastry Roller
IN THE
English Treen Tradition

Fig. 12-1. A traditional turned and whittled roller. Note how all parts come together to make a single compact whole.

Treen, a Saxon word that means "of the trees" or "from the trees," by modern definition refers to just about any small wooden, turned, or carved article; that is, an article which is small enough to be picked up in one hand. For example, snuff boxes, platters, egg cups, toys, and games boards, if they are made of wood, they might be described as treen.

Treen has, for many people, come to mean specifically all the small turned and carved items that were once used in kitchens, laundries, keeping rooms, and dairies. Wooden bowls, plates, milk ladles, butter molds, butter prints, plate racks, food boxes, carriers, salt boxes, clothes rollers, kegs, stools, candle holders, string boxes, mangle boards, spoon racks, and jiggers—they are all examples of treen. Of all these items, perhaps the most beautiful and evocative are the food rollers and molds (FIG. 12-1). These little presses, rollers, prints, molds, and stamps come in a great many shapes and types. There are biscuit stamps that have figures and motifs carved in incised line. There are little butter molds that have carved designs on the inside, the idea being to pack the butter tightly in the box, and then to carefully remove the pegged and hinged sides. There are cheese pressers with carved coats of arms, and so I could continue.

Best of all, and certainly the most decorative, are the little carved pastry and butter rollers. Turned in lime, sycamore, and boxwood, and skillfully carved with the most delicate incised and relief designs, these rollers are reminders of times gone by. It is difficult to believe that there was a time, not so long ago, when just about every village had one or two woodworkers who were willing and able to turn their hands to the whole range of woodworking skills, and a time when our grandmothers and great-grandmothers could spend many hours decorating pastries, pies, and butter pats.

Materials

A piece of sycamore, lime, or boxwood 2½x2½ inches square and about 12 inches long
A small quantity of PVA glue
A small quantity of vegetable oil

Tools

A short length of dowel
Work-out paper, tracing paper, pencils
A small lathe
A set of turning gouges
A ruler
A pair of calipers
A small, straight saw
A coping saw
A small hand drill with a ¼-inch and a ⅜-inch bit
A set of small wood-carving gouges
A bench and vise
A pack of graded sandpapers

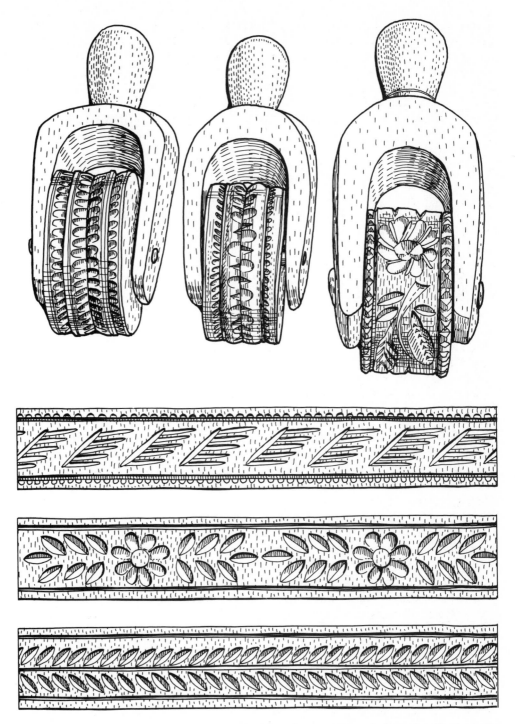

Fig. 12-2. Inspirational designs—three characteristic rollers and three design strips. See how all the designs have been cut and worked with the minimum of strokes.

DESIGN AND TECHNIQUE

Before you start this project, have a good look at the various inspirational drawings (FIG. 12-2) and then visit a folk museum that has a collection of eighteenth and/or nineteenth century kitchen and dairy utensils and items. Focus your attention on the butter and pastry-making molds, presses, and rollers.

When you see rollers of the small stirrup type, as illustrated (they might be called pastry or butter rollers) have a close-up look and see how they have been worked and put together. Note how the handle-and-fork frame has been turned out of one piece, and see how the turning has been cut so that it has two flat faces. If possible, have a look at the handle end on, and see how the two cut-away flat faces have been worked so that they take full advantage of the run of the grain. Also, if you get the chance, use a piece of soft putty or modeling paste to make rolled impressions.

Noting all the variations in frame design—meaning some rollers have long, slender, spindle-worked handles, while others have short handles and long prongs—take your work-out paper and a soft pencil, and make a series of design sketches and working drawings (FIG. 12-3). Note the diameter of the wheel, the width of the forked stirrup, the diameter of the pivot pin, the loose fit of the wheel on the pin, and so on. Finally, make a series of detailed studies of the carved designs and see how invariably the patterns and motifs have been cut-in and worked so that the resultant pressed designs stand out in high relief.

Turning the Main Form

Check that your lathe is in good order, make sure that you have a choice piece of wood, arrange your various tools so that they are comfortably at hand, then set your piece of prepared wood between centers. Using the tools of your choice, turn a cylindrical blank that is about 2 inches in diameter. This done, measure and step off the length of the handle, the length of the forked frame, and the thickness of the wheel.

With one eye on the measured drawings (FIG. 12-4), take caliper readings and turn off the various swellings, necks, and grooves that go to make up the delicate form (FIG. 12-5). This done, part-off the wheel thickness, turn the wheel beads, part-off the main form, and then take the wood to a good, smooth finish (FIG. 12-6). NOTE: if you are a raw beginner, it might be as well at this stage to turn off three or four spare wheels. You can use them for practice when you start carving.

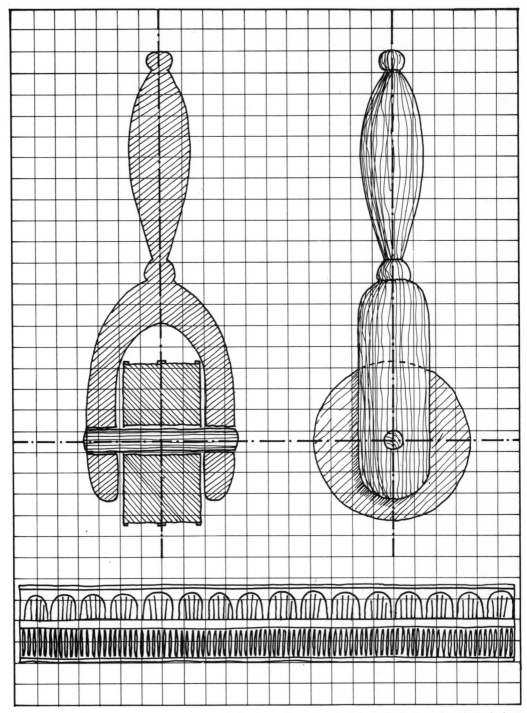

Fig. 12-3. Working drawings—the grid scale is about 4 squares to 1 inch. Note how the pivot pin is a tight fit in the stirrup and a loose fit in the roller. The design needs to be well considered so that it fits the roller without a gap or overlap.

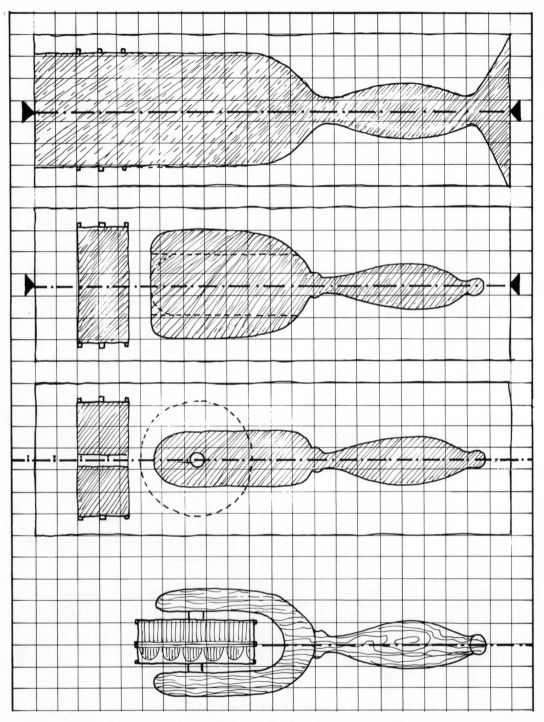

Fig. 12-4. From top to bottom, cross sections showing the order of work. See how the curved shoulders of the large turned form need to be sliced away to make the stirrup.

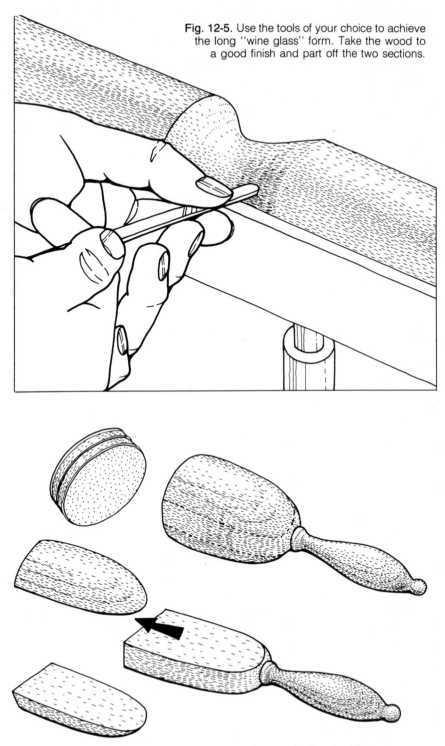

Fig. 12-5. Use the tools of your choice to achieve the long "wine glass" form. Take the wood to a good finish and part off the two sections.

Fig. 12-6. Part off the roller disk, and cut away the shoulders.

Cutting the Pronged Stirrup
and Drilling the Pivot Holes

When you get the wheel and the handled form back to the workbench, check them against your working drawings with a measure and a pair of calipers. If all is well, secure the handled form in the jaws of a muffled vise, note the direction of the grain, and then set-out the thickness of the stirrup prongs accordingly.

When you are sure that all is correct, use a straight saw to clear away the two areas of waste from either side of the prongs. When you have achieved two smooth, flat faces, mark off the position of the wheel and use the hand drill and the ¼-inch bit to work the pivot hole (FIG. 12-7).

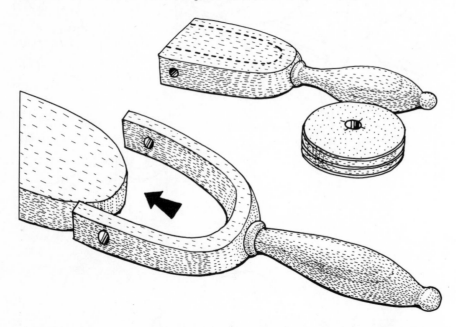

Fig. 12-7. When you have achieved a nicely worked stirrup blank, drill the pivot holes through the blank and the wheel, then clear away the waste from inside the stirrup.

This done, take a compass, pencil, and measure, and draw in the curve that sets out the inside prong profile. Again check with your working drawings, then set the wood in the vise and use the coping saw to clear away the waste. Work at a steady pace, especially when you come to the relatively delicate short-grained areas at the top of the curve. Make sure that you don't force or twist the saw.

When you have cut out the rather delicate pronged form, take the graded sandpapers and work the wood to a good, smooth, round-edged finish. Finally, take the hand drill and the ⅜-inch bit and bore a hole through the center of the wheel.

Carving the Wheel Patterns and Designs

Have a look at our inspirational designs and see how the carved patterns tend to be relatively simple. That is to say, they are nearly always just a series of direct and uncomplicated gouge nicks that suggest wheat sheaves, flowers, and such. NOTE: if you are a beginner it might be as well to have a try-out with one or other of your spare wheels.

Having selected one of our designs or one of your own museum studies, take your wheel, a soft pencil, and a small strip of tracing paper, and set about pencil-press transferring the design through to the working face of the wood. If you have difficulties spacing the design by eye, use a compass and a flexible tape measure, and divide the circumference of the wheel up into short, well-defined, easy-to-work areas.

When you come to the actual carving, place the wheel so that one or other of the flat sides is resting on the bench, and then approach the face to be carved with short, controlled stabbing cuts (FIG. 12-8). Support the little wheel, and guide the shaft of your chosen gouge with one hand, pushing down with the other.

See how our design is made up from a series of gouge scoops and a running band of V-tool cuts. As you work, cut down and use the beadings as stop cuts.

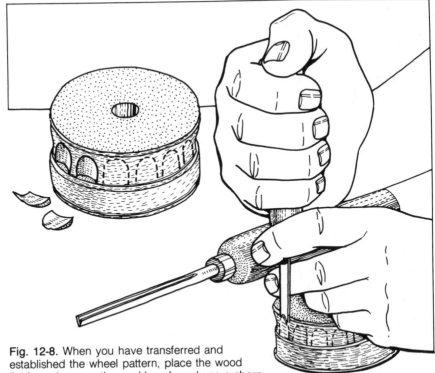

Fig. 12-8. When you have transferred and established the wheel pattern, place the wood flat-face down on the workbench and use a sharp, deep-section gouge to cut and work the beautiful and characteristic fluted designs.

Don't try to work at speed; just carve at a steady pace and be ready to pull short if you feel the blade running out of control or digging too deeply into the grain. The waste wood should come away as smooth curls or chips; however, if the wood starts to cut rough, then either change the direction of your cut or spend time bringing the tool to a good edge on the oilstone.

Continue, first working the large gouge scoops, and then surface-decorating both the scoops and the flat areas with the fine V-cuts. When you have achieved what you consider is a good design, then run the wheel over a piece of modeling paste or maybe a scrap of pastry to take a few impressions. Finally trim the wood to a good fit and finish.

PUTTING TOGETHER

When you have carved the wheel, take the short length of ¼-inch-diameter dowel and position the wheel between the prongs of the stirrup. Being careful that you don't twist or force the dowel, pass the dowel through the holes. If all is well, the dowel should be tight fit in the prongs and a loose fit in the wheel. When you are pleased with the fit, withdraw the dowel slightly, dab a little glue in the prong holes, and then push it home. Finally, pare the ends of the dowel with a sharp knife, wipe the wood over with a little vegetable oil, and the job is done.

• When you are choosing your timber, be sure to reject wood that is knotty or wood that has a twisted grain.

• When you are carving the patterns and motifs, go for the simplest forms. Let the tool cuts suggest their own designs.

• If you are going to use the roller in the kitchen, be sure that you don't wipe the finished roller over with a spirit or a machine oil. If in doubt, use a dab of butter or cooking oil.

PROJECT 13

MAKING A *Nursery Comfort Board*
IN THE
English and American Tradition

Fig. 13-1. A traditional comfort board.

Known variously as *dummy boards*, *comfort boards*, *dummy silhouettes*, *dummy valet boards*, and even just *figure boards*, these life-size wooden figures were quite a common household item in seventeenth, eighteenth, and early nineteenth century England and America (FIG. 13-1). Made from flat plank or slab wood, cut out like a silhouette, and then painted on one or both sides, these beautiful, bold, primitive figures were thought at one time to be mere whimsies that had no real use other than that of being amusing and decorative.

Of course, in many ways the various names do speak for themselves. For example, dummy boards were used as life-size shop signs; that is to say, they were painted and decorated so as to advertise a garment or product. Valet boards were designed to hold a tray, a small container, or even items of clothes. Figure boards were considered to be lifelike images that could be used as a screen to protect the user from draughts or from the direct heat of a fire.

Perhaps the most interesting and evocative of all these boards are the uniquely beautiful little figures of children that are known as comfort boards. These little figures were made for nurseries and used in the same way as a child might now use a nightlight or a teddy bear. That is to say, comfort figures were considered by children to be friendly, comforting companions. So just as now on a long, dark, spooky night a lonely child might look at a favorite picture book, cuddle a doll, or just enjoy being surrounded by familiar toys and nursery items, so a child in an eighteenth century English grand house, or a child in a midnineteenth century New Hampshire farmstead drew comfort from his dummy or comfort figure.

Of course, in many ways comfort boards are one better than dolls and picture books in that they were painted so that they actually looked like a brother, a sister, or some such. It is on record that dummy board figures were made and painted by the same tradesmen who made and painted family portraits, overmantel pictures, and chimney boards.

Materials

A sheet of good-quality, exterior-grade ½-to ¾-inch-thick
multilayer plywood, of a size to suit
A block of wood for the base (see working drawings and details)
A small tin of filler, a small tin of knotting
A tin each of size white emulsion paint and artist's varnish
A set of artist's oil colors
Turpentine
A small quantity of linseed oil

Tools

A coping saw, a straight saw
A pack of graded sandpapers
Work-out paper, tracing paper
Broad and fine-point artist's brushes
A mixing board or palette
Usual workshop items like cloths, a bench, and plenty of newspaper

DESIGN AND TECHNIQUE

Before you start this project, visit a museum of folk art, and view examples of comfort figures, dummy boards, and "everyday" pictures and portraits that were painted in England and America between 1780 and 1860 (FIGS. 13-2 and 13-3). By *everyday*, we mean pictures painted by itinerant artists, stencilers, and decorators, and by self-taught rural artists, limners, or portraitists.

Spend a long time just looking at these paintings and studying their style. See the refreshing, uninhibited directness of the figures, the use of bold colors and firm outlines, the absence of what we understand as "good" design, and most important of all, the almost childlike treatment of features like eyes and mouths. See how although most of these paintings fail when it comes to correct anatomy and perspective, nevertheless there is about them an intenseness and a feeling that the artist has caught the spirit of the portrait and the mood of the period.

Of course, from our informed twentieth-century standpoint, it is very difficult to achieve paintings that have about them a quality of innocence, but make a series of notes and sketches. Record colors and dress details, and also try to analyze just what it is about the figures/pictures that makes them so attractively primitive. Finally, collect museum handouts—meaning catalogs and postcards—and if possible start a collection of magazine clips. With a project of this character, it is necessary that you do your very best to become absorbed in the atmosphere and feeling of the subject.

Fig. 13-2. Inspirational design— a very early comfort/dummy board, life size.

Fig. 13-3. Inspirational designs taken from primitive folk paintings

Boy with Finch,
John Brewster,
c. 1800

Little Girl in Red,
Ammi Phillips,
c. 1834-36

Child with Peach,
c. 1700

Girl with lemon

Fig. 13-4. Working drawings—scale to suit. It is best to make it life size. Note how in section the board is slotted into and supported by a baulk wood base.

Fretting Out the Figure and Preparation

When you get back to your workshop, pin all your sketches and collected material up around your working area. Set your sheet of plywood out on the work surface and check it over to make sure that it is free from splits, lamination bubbles and breaks, and insect attack.

Make a well-worked drawing of your chosen figure (FIG. 13-4), and then with pencil and tracing paper, transfer the figure outline or profile through to the working face of your wood. At this stage, don't transfer all the small dress and face details, just work the main silhouette outline.

When you have achieved a well-established outline, set the wood up on the workbench and, with straight saw and coping saw, fret out the figure. Note the extra wood at the feet for the base-slab mounting.

When you have cut the figure out, clear away all unnecessary tools and clutter, then set-to with a block and the graded sandpaper, and rub the cut edges of the plywood down to a smooth, round finish. Now mix a small amount of filler, work it into the rounded edge, wait for it to dry, and then cut back with the sandpaper until the edge of the ply looks perfectly smooth.

Fig. 13-5. When the cut profile has been prepared, lay on a well-brushed primer coat, draw in the main color-area outlines, and then block them in with paint. It is best to lay on washes of turpentine-thinned color.

This done, give the wood, back and front, a couple of well-brushed coats of size and leave it to dry. Finally, with a broad, flat brush, lay on a couple of coats of white water-based emulsion, and once again put the wood to one side to dry.

Transferring the Design and Blocking In

When the white emulsion is completely dry, swiftly rub it down to remove whiskers of wood grain. Now tape the tracing in place with tabs of masking tape, and pencil-press transfer all the traced lines through to the emulsion-covered surface. When all the lines have been transferred, go over them with a hard pencil and make sure that they are all clearly set-in.

Now refresh your eye by having a look at your chosen design and your color notes. List the colors and then squeeze a little of each out onto your palette. Select one of the main design areas—say the dress—take a little of the chosen color, mix it with a little turpentine, and then lay on a thin, even coat (FIG. 13-5). At this stage, don't bother with any details, for example where the straps of the bag cross over the dress. Just block-in the main chunks of color, the bodice, the sleeves, and the full skirt. Continue to set out the hair, the face, the bag, the book, and the shoes (FIG. 13-6).

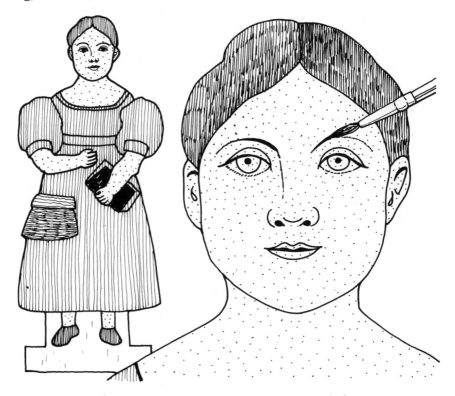

Fig. 13-6. Use a fine brush to define the main features.

Applying the Shadow and Tone

When you have covered all the design areas with washes of turpentine-thinned color, put the work to one side to dry. When the paint is dry, have another look at your design. Then go over your figure board reestablishing the pencil-drawn lines and details.

Now before you go any further, take a pencil and very lightly frame the areas of dark, shadow, or tone. For example, one side of the head, one side of the bag, one side of the dress and so on will all be in shadow. Establish these areas, then mix up a batch of slightly darker colors—that is, add more pigment, and a little oil and turpentine—and go over the painting, blocking in the shadow or tone (FIG. 13-7). Don't fuss about trying to mix subtle blends of color, just use raw colors straight from the tube, and build up the forms with thin color washes or glazes, as described.

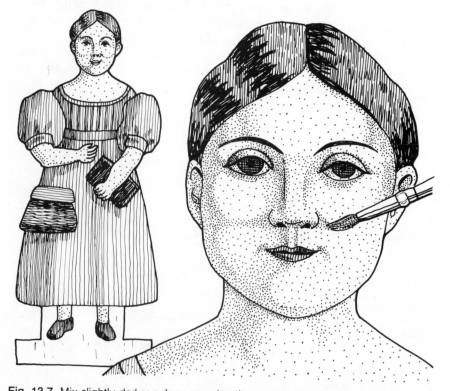

Fig. 13-7. Mix slightly darker colors, meaning the same colors but less turpentine, and paint in the areas of shadow.

Have a look at the project picture, and see how, as in general terms the figure is lit from the right, so the areas of shadow or darker tone occur on the left: on the hair, down one side of each of the sleeves, down the side of the bodice and the skirt, and so on. Of course, the book and the bag also have their own cast shadows. Keep all this in mind as you gradually build up the darker areas.

Applying the Light Colors

Have another look at the project picture and see how, just as one side of the figure is in shadow, so the other side is in light. That is to say, the figure is lit from the right.

Mix another batch of the base colors, but this time add just a little white. Now, working down the right-hand side of the figure, lighten the hair, the side of the cheeks and the nose, the sleeves, and so forth (FIG. 13-8). Don't overdo either the dark shadows or the light areas; just aim little by little to build up the thin washes or glazes until the whole form looks to be rounded and three-dimensional.

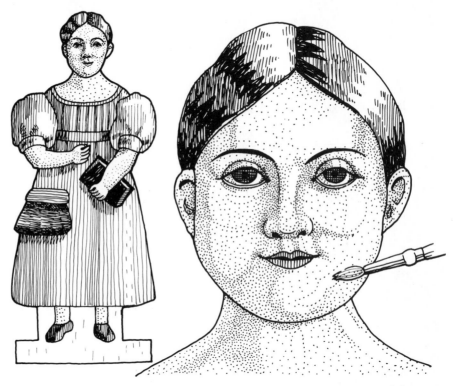

Fig. 13-8. Using a turpentine-thinned color mix and just a little white, apply the light areas.

THE DETAILS, HIGHLIGHTS, VARNISHING, AND FINISHING

When the base colors have dried, mix small amounts of dense, thick color and set about lining in the details. So you might line-in the eye brows, the nose, the chin, the trim around the neck of the dress, the edges of the book, the handles of the bag, and so forth (FIG. 13-9).

As you are working these small areas, try to achieve a "thick paint" quality. For example, when you are detailing the locket or the ribbon, actually build up

Fig. 13-9. Finally, detail and highlight the eyes, ribbons, and fingernails.

the paint thickness so that it stands out slightly from the ground. When you have worked the details, use the smallest amount of white and a fine brush, and go over the whole figure, picking out the highlights. That is to say, dot-in the pupils of the eyes, pick out the curve of the lips, and give the hair its sheen.

When you have achieved a fair likeness, then put the board to one side to dry. Wait until the paint is completely dry—and this might take some considerable time, depending on just how much oil you added to your paint—then take a broad brush and lay on a couple of coats of varnish. Finally, fit and fix the base, as shown in the working drawings, and the job is done.

- Be sparing with both the oil and the turpentine. Too much oil sets back the paint-drying time, and too much turpentine results in flat color. Go for the middle way.

- If you want to speed up the project, use either acrylics or water colors, rather than oil paints.

- Try not to overwork or "polish" the forms. For example, although modern art books recommend that on no account should you use raw colors or raw white for the highlights, in this instance ignore such advice. In fact, try to achieve a bold, amateurish, untutored feel to the work.

PROJECT 14

MAKING AN
Oval Steam-bent Carrier
IN THE
American Shaker Tradition

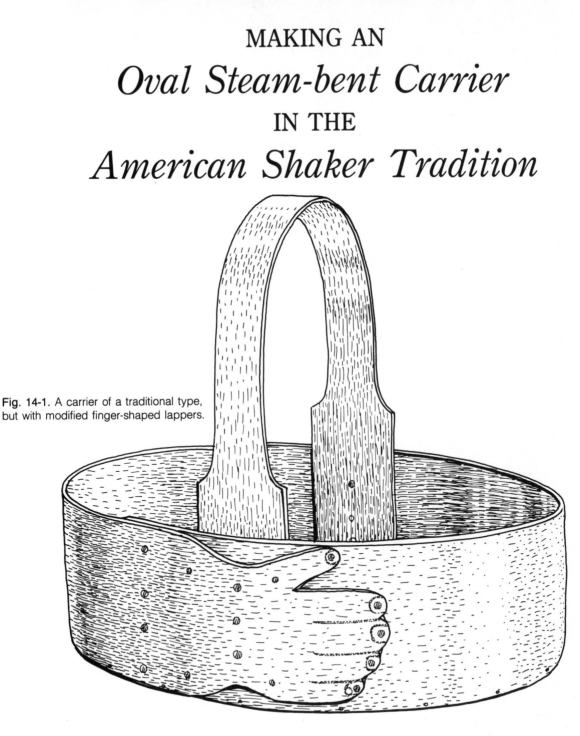

Fig. 14-1. A carrier of a traditional type, but with modified finger-shaped lappers.

"Hands to work and hearts to God," was the guiding motto of the Shakers, a dissident group of Quakers who settled in America toward the end of the eighteenth century. Led by their founding prophetess, Mother Ann Lee, and then later by her successor, Father James Whittaker, the group established a commune at Niskeyuna (now Watervliet, New York). By the end of the nineteenth century, there were eighteen such communities and a Shaker population of about 6,000.

The Shaker's philosophy of honesty before God, and their sincere desire to use to the full what they considered to be God-given talents resulted in them endeavoring to create products that were honest, simple, dignified, and functional. Another Shaker injunction was to "Build as though you were to live for a thousand years, and as you would do if you knew you were going to die tomorrow." So it was that Shaker woodworkers created all manner of wonderfully crafted pieces of furniture and items of domestic woodware. Chairs, tables, cupboards, clocks, beds, boxes, and chests were all built as "prayers and offerings." It has been said of the Shaker craftsmen that not only did they work for God, but that they also worked with God.

Perhaps the most characteristic of all Shaker-made pieces are the oval steam-bent boxes and carriers (FIG. 14-1). Made variously of maple, birch, and cherry, such boxes were worked by steaming and bending thin slats of wood around molds, and then gluing and nailing the resultant hoops to bottoms of thicker wood. Made singly and also in nested sets, some boxes with lids and others with handles, some left plain and others colored with milk paints (FIG. 14-2), these beautiful utilitarian forms are so delicate, sensitive, and so obviously worked with a diligent striving to create "something perfect unto its purpose," that they have come to symbolize the simple, honest Shaker way of life.

Materials

A piece of prepared ½-inch-thick, 8-x-6-inch pine
Two ⅛-inch-thick slats of cherry or birch veneer:
One piece at about 24 inches long and 2½ inches wide
One piece at about 16 inches long and 2 inches wide
15 copper rivets
PVA adhesive
A number of dolly pegs

Tools

A sheet of stiff card
Work-out paper, tracing paper, pencils
12 copper nails
A hand drill and bits to suit the size of the rivets and nails
A small hammer
A workbench
A vise
A homemade pipe anvil (see illustration details)

(. . . continued)

A metal straightedge

A scalpel

A coping saw or an electric fretsaw

A wood-burning tool or an electric soldering iron

Graded sandpapers

A heavy craft knife

A kettle and steamer, as illustrated or one to your own design

A mold, as illustrated in the working drawing

A pair of heat-proof gloves

DESIGN AND TECHNIQUE

First have a look at the working drawings (FIG. 14-3) and consider just how the carrier has been worked and put together. See how the *lappers*, or *fingers*, have actually been modified and shaped so that they look like a hand, and see how the hoop has been overlapped and fixed with copper rivets. Note also how the handle has been delicately shaped and riveted to the hooped sides, and how in turn the hooped sides have been fixed to the base with copper nails.

When you have considered all the tool, material, and technique implications of the project, then take a trip to your nearest folk museum. Get to see not only Shaker boxes and carriers, but also those made in eighteenth and nineteenth century England, Sweden, and Poland.

Making and Using the Templates

When you have studied all the available material—museum pieces, photographs in magazines and such—and when you have considered possible design, size, and material modifications, then make a full-size working drawing.

This done, take tracings from the master design, and then pencil-press transfer the traced lines through to the working face of the stiff card. You will need to make templates for all three parts: the base, the main side strip, and the handle. NOTE: if you have doubts as to the proportions of the carrier when it is made up, then make a prototype using thin card and staples.

When you have adjusted the template profiles to suit your own design needs, take a scalpel and a straightedge, and cut out the three templates. Now set your wood out on the work surface and check it over for faults. Make sure that the base wood is free from loose knots and splits, and see that the handle and side strips have a straight grain and are free from curl, stains, and splits. Reject all wood that looks to be less than perfect.

When you are happy that all is correct and as described, then take the templates and transfer their profiles to the wood. Finally, use a soft pencil to label the right side of the wood—that is to say, the outside of the carrier.

Fig. 14-2. Inspirational designs—(*top left*) A nesting set of Shaker food boxes; (*top right*) An American box made of whale bone and wood, 5½ inches high, made about 1850; (*bottom*) A Shaker box, 5¾ inches long, unusual in that it is signed, dated, and carved.

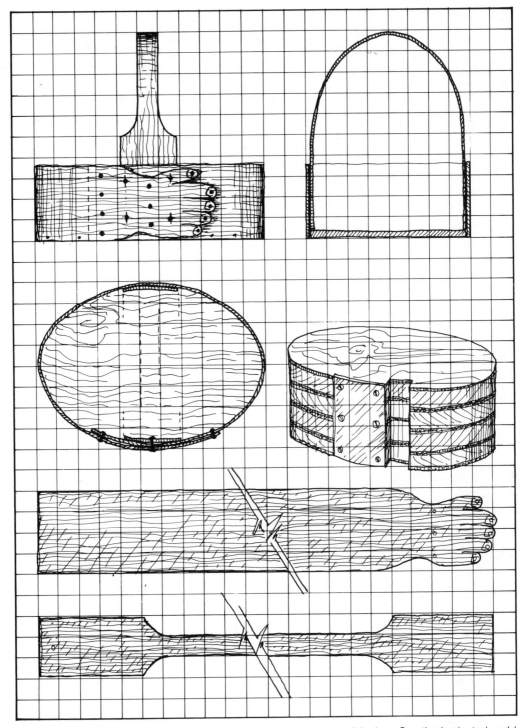

Fig. 14-3. Working drawings—the grid scale is about 3 squares to 2 inches. See the laminated mold and note the inset metal anvil plate.

Cutting the Blanks

When you have used the templates to establish the profiles, secure the wood, one piece at a time, in the vise, and then set to work with the coping saw (FIG. 14-4). Steady and turn the wood with one hand, and guide and maneuver the coping saw with the other. Aim to cut on the waste side of the pencil line. As you are cutting, try to keep the saw blade at right angles to the working face of the wood. Continue until you have achieved three crisply worked, clean-cut blanks.

NOTE: take extra care when you are cutting out the side strip. Only round-off the end of the fingertips. Don't cut in between the fingers.

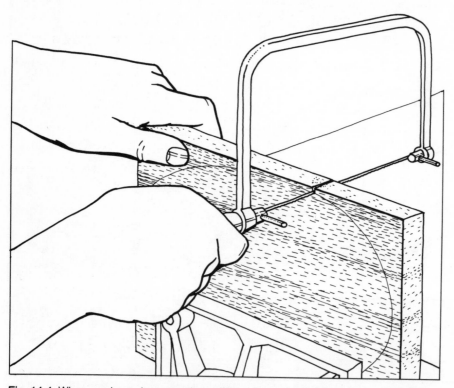

Fig. 14-4. When you have drawn out the profiles, use a coping saw to cut out the blanks.

Tapering and Decorating the Lappers

First of all, have a look at the working drawings and details, and see how the ends of the carrier-hoop overlap. Noting the amount of overlap, set your strip of wood out on the workbench so that the outside is uppermost. Now take the rasp, have another last check just to make sure that you are going to taper what will be the inside of the hoop overlap, then set to work. Taper and feather the last 6 inches at the tail end of the strip, and work the wood until you have reduced the ⅛-inch thickness by at least one-quarter.

Now, with the wood still outside uppermost, take the scalpel and the sandpaper, and tidy up the hand profile. Rub down all the rough edges, splinters, and burrs.

Next, switch on the wood-burning tool, allow it to heat to a dullish red, just short of red hot, then go to work. Line-in between the fingers, draw in the nail curves, and generally decorate as you think fit (FIG. 14-5).

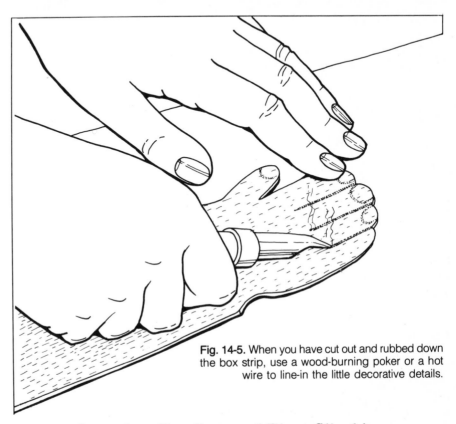

Fig. 14-5. When you have cut out and rubbed down the box strip, use a wood-burning poker or a hot wire to line-in the little decorative details.

Steaming, Bending, and Rivet-Clinching

First have a good look at our steamer and mold, as illustrated. See how the steamer is a very simple homemade plywood box-and-boiler affair. Note how the mold is built like a sandwich from exterior-grade plywood. See also how there is a stainless steel plate let flush into the side of the mold. Then build similar items to suit your own needs. (See the *Workshop Data* section.)

Next, place the side strip into the steamer and leave it for about 15 to 20 minutes (FIG. 14-6). When the wood has been well steamed and is flexible, take it out of the steamer, wrap it tightly around the mold, and then clamp it up with the dolly pegs or a clamp (FIG. 14-7). When the wood has cooled and set to shape, take it off the mold, smear the inside of the overlap with PVA glue, and then clamp up. Using a modified mold (make a bridge form), steam and shape the handle in like manner.

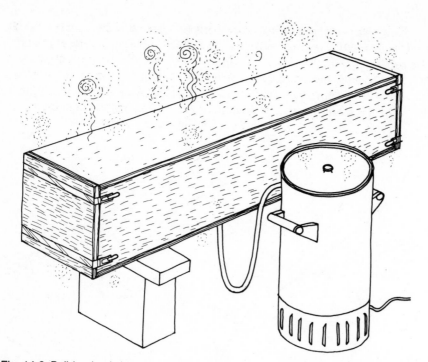

Fig. 14-6. Build a simple box-and-boiler steamer and steam the wood to be bent for about 15 to 20 minutes.

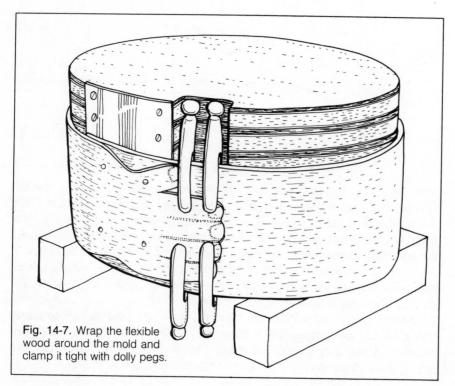

Fig. 14-7. Wrap the flexible wood around the mold and clamp it tight with dolly pegs.

While the handle is cooling and setting to shape, drill pilot holes through the hoop overlap, drive four nails through the holes, and peen them against the stainless steel mold plate (FIG. 14-8). That is to say, drive the copper nails through the two layers of wood until the points of the nails mushroom-rivet and clinch the hoop. Now remove the hoop from the mold and drill pilot holes through the rivet points at wrist and fingertips. Finally support the hoop on the pipe anvil and then rivet, mushroom, and clinch, as already described.

Fig. 14-8. Drill, place, position, and clinch the copper rivets.

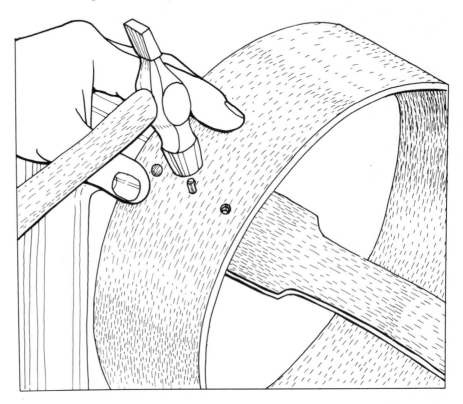

The Handle and Base

When the hoop has been clinched, cut the steam-bent handle to size, and trim to a good fit. Now, allowing for the thickness of the oval base, place the ends of the handle inside the hoop and mark, drill, and rivet. When this has been done, place the hoop on the oval base, mark off the inside profile, and then modify the shape of the base with the coping saw.

Now rub down to a good, tight fit, drill pilot holes around the bottom edge of the hoop, fit the base so that it abuts the bottom ends of the handle and is contained by the hoop, and then drive the copper nails home. Finally, rub the whole carrier down with a fine-grade sandpaper, and the job is done.

- At the start of the project, it is most important that you choose your wood with care. Twisted, slanting grain might result in uneven bending or breaks. Be warned.

- Some box-makers soak the wood prior to steaming.

- You might use long-nosed clamps, rather than dolly pegs.

- The finished carrier can be waxed or painted. (See the *Workshop Data* section.)

PROJECT 15

MAKING A
Hanging Shelf
IN THE
English and American Tradition

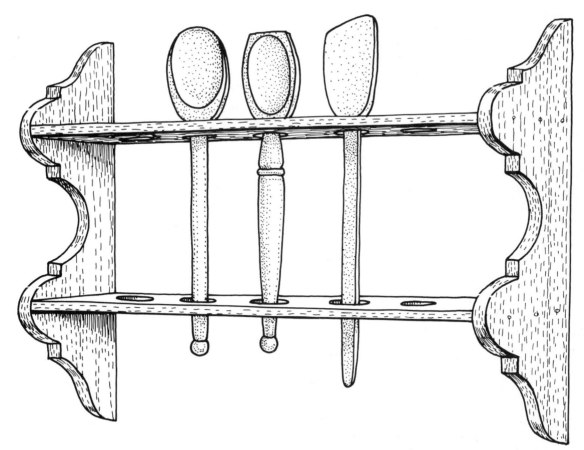

Fig. 15-1. A traditional rack with cyma-curved end boards.

Our forefathers were particularly imaginative when it came to making such ordinary utility items as wall racks and shelves. They didn't worry too much about size, fixings, and fancy joints. One gets the impression that they just searched out a few scraps of timber and then set-to with unrestrained gusto. Not for them any preconceived overworked ideas about correct style, color matching, and other such faddy notions. If they needed a shelf to keep the spoons or plates off the floor (they didn't have many cupboards), they just made one as the mood took them.

That these primitive country cottage craftsmen enjoyed their work is only too obvious when one sees examples of wall racks and shelves in country museums and show houses. They are beautiful, spontaneous designs: shelves with proud, full-curved side boards; racks with carved, pierced, and scalloped front boards; and so on. Spoon racks of the shelf type—that is to say racks that are made up from one or two pierced spoon strips set between a couple of shaped side boards—are essentially kitchen hearth pieces, meaning that they were usually a one-off made by the man of the house to answer a particular need (FIG. 15-1). It is the very fact that they are one-offs that gives them their friendly, rustic, unique individuality.

Of course, such shelves and racks were made all over—in England, Scotland and Wales, in Europe, and in colonial America—and so consequently there are many, many different types (FIG. 15-2). In nineteenth century Wales, they favored racks with fancy chip-carved backboards all cut and decorated in the manner of Welsh love spoons. In eighteenth and nineteenth century Poland they put all the design work into a carved and pierced strip that they used to cover up the shelf edge. In colonial America, they tended to have very exuberant plunging and scalloped side boards and shelves let into openended housing grooves. Whether they be plain, fancy, wildly ornate, or just functional, racks and shelves of the country cottage type are characteristically honest and uninhibited in both design and construction.

Materials

A quantity of prepared smooth-grained white pine:
One piece at ¾ inch thick, 24 inches long, and 5 inches wide
One piece at ½ inch thick, 24 inches long, and 5 inches wide
A handfull of panel pins
A small quantity of PVA glue
Acrylic color to suit

Tools

A coping or bow saw
A small straight saw
A ½-inch flat chisel
A brace
A 1-inch-diameter drill bit
A compass
A pencil, work-out paper, tracing paper

(. . . continued)

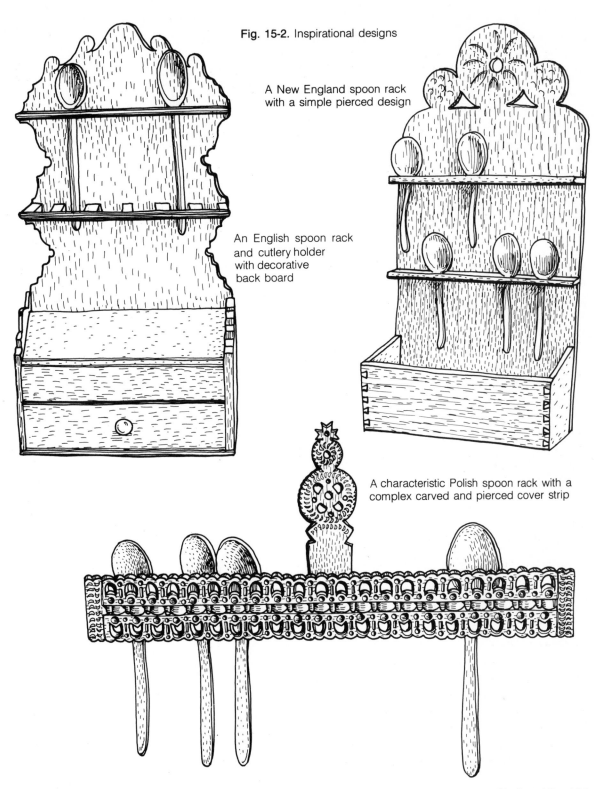

Fig. 15-2. Inspirational designs

A New England spoon rack with a simple pierced design

An English spoon rack and cutlery holder with decorative back board

A characteristic Polish spoon rack with a complex carved and pierced cover strip

A ruler measure
A small hammer
A square
A C-clamp
Card and scissors
A small quantity of dried milk powder
A broad flat brush

DESIGN AND TECHNIQUE

Before you start this project, study little wall shelves and racks that were made before the turn of the century. Visit a folk museum or an antique shop that specializes in kitchen hearth furniture, or better still, visit an aged relation or friend who lives in a farmhouse and who favors country rustic items.

When you get to see examples of this type of furniture, take a close-up look at the way they have been put together. Note how characteristically the shelves are notched into slotted open-ended housing joints and then held with pins. See also how sometimes such humble shelves are made out of packing-case wood, or even made up from scraps salvaged from other pieces of furniture. Consider the various designs, take note of the way they have been put together, see how the designs relate to the period in which they are made, and so on.

When you have some appreciation of all the tool, technique, and material implications of making such an item, then take your work-out paper and a soft pencil, and sketch out features, designs, and details that you would like to work into your piece. Pay particular attention to the shaped end boards. Make sure that your sketches show sizes, joint details, etc.

Finally, have a look at as many magazine pictures and museum handouts as possible. Maybe start a collection of inspirational designs and illustrations.

Designing and Making the Template

When you get your sketches and inspirational material back to the workshop, pin them up around your working areas. Now before you actually put tool to wood, spend time deciding how you want your shelf to be. Is it going to be a spoon rack? Is it going to be a plate shelf? Are the ends going to be pierced and carved, as well as shaped? All these points need to be carefully considered.

This done, make a full-size measured working drawing (FIG. 15-3). Now take your cardboard—it is best to use thin scraps of carton card—cut it to the size of the end boards, fold it in half and in half again, and then play around with a pencil and a pair of scissors until you come up with a suitable profile. You will soon see that by folding, cutting, and then opening out the card, it is possible to work out any number of interesting and exciting end-board designs.

When you have made a suitable cardboard template, put it on one side and check your wood for faults. Reject wood that is sappy or split, but in this instance don't necessarily discard wood that is stained, old, salvaged, or knotty, but rather see how these features might be used to enhance the total design.

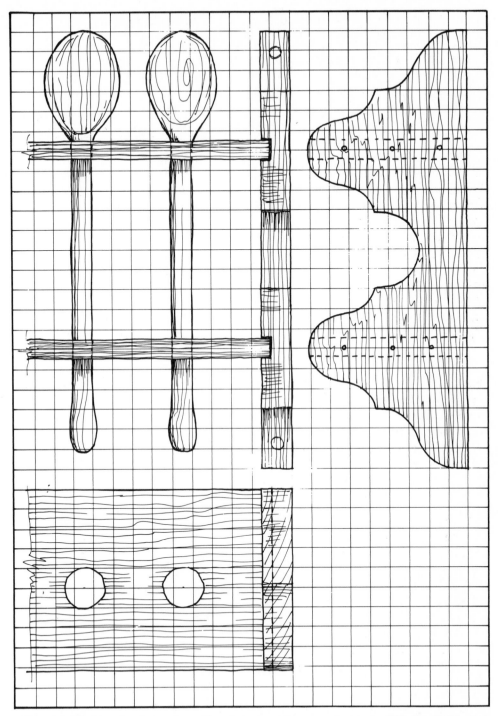

Fig. 15-3. Working drawings—the grid scale is about 2 squares to 1 inch. Note the shelf-to-end channel housing.

Cutting the Wood to Size and Setting Out

When you are happy with your master design and the materials, then use the square, pencil, and the straight saw to cut the wood down into four 12-inch lengths. You need two shelf pieces at ½ inch thick and a little less than 4 inches wide, and two end boards at ¾ inch thick and about 5 inches wide.

Have a look at your working drawings. Note such factors as the spacing of the spoon holes and the placing of the two shelves in relation to the end boards; then use the pencil and the template to set the wood out accordingly. Draw around the template, mark out the position of the shelf housing slot and the spoon holes, then label the wood "end 1," "end 2," "top shelf," and so on (FIG. 15-4). Check that all the measurements are just right, then clear the work surface of all clutter and set out your tools.

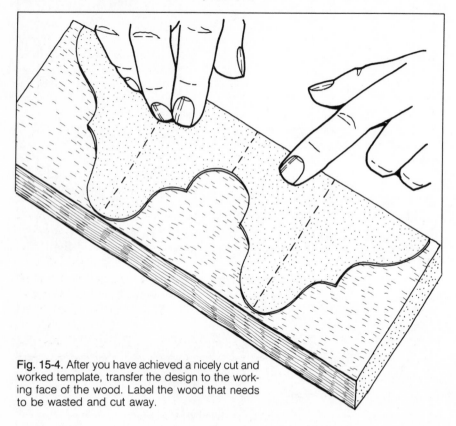

Fig. 15-4. After you have achieved a nicely cut and worked template, transfer the design to the working face of the wood. Label the wood that needs to be wasted and cut away.

Working the End Boards

Make sure that the housing joint slots are correctly placed. With the wood held securely in the bench vise or up against a bench stop, use the square, the straight saw, and the chisel to clear open-ended shelf trenches that are ½ inch wide and about ¼ inch deep (FIG. 15-5). Cut and work both boards.

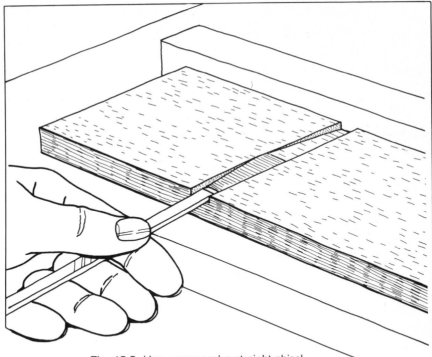

Fig. 15-5. Use a saw and a straight chisel to clear the housing joint slot/channel. Cut and work the slot so that the shelves are a good fit.

This done, check that the template line is clearly drawn in, and sandwich the two end boards so that they are face to face, as illustrated. Now with the two boards held securely in the vise, use the coping or bow saw to cut out the rather delicate curved profile (FIG. 15-6). Work the saw with a good, steady, even stroke, trying all the while to keep the blade and the angle of cut at 90 degrees to the working face of the wood. NOTE: cutting the proud curves is a little tricky because you do have to be a bit careful that you don't knock off areas of short grain.

When you have cleared the waste from the two identical mirror-image profiles, take a scrap of fine sandpaper and rub down all cut edges until they are smooth and round-cornered to the touch.

Making the Shelves

First slide the two shelf lengths into the end-board housing trenches and make sure that they are a good fit. If necessary, rub down the shelf end thickness. When the fit is square and firm, have a look at your various wooden kitchen spoons and servers. Measure the thickness of the handles and the width and depth of the spoon bowls, and set out the position of the line of holes accordingly (FIG. 15-7).

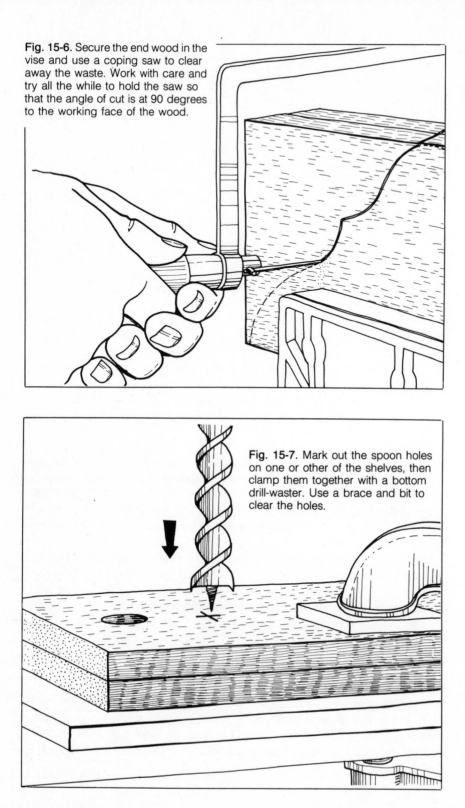

Fig. 15-6. Secure the end wood in the vise and use a coping saw to clear away the waste. Work with care and try all the while to hold the saw so that the angle of cut is at 90 degrees to the working face of the wood.

Fig. 15-7. Mark out the spoon holes on one or other of the shelves, then clamp them together with a bottom drill-waster. Use a brace and bit to clear the holes.

When you have established the position of the holes, then, as with the two end boards, sandwich the two shelves face to face, as illustrated. This time, however, add a drill waster to the underside of the sandwich. Check that all is as described, then clamp the sandwich to the bench and use the brace and bit to bore the spoon holes. Finally, separate the sandwich and use a little scrap of sandpaper to rub down the front of the shelves and the edges of the cut holes.

PUTTING TOGETHER, FINISHING, AND PAINTING

Clear the workbench and set the shelves between the two boards. Make sure that all four boards are the right way around and well placed. When you are happy that all is correct, remove one of the end boards, dribble a little PVA glue into the shelf housing, then very carefully replace the end board and tap three or four pins through the joints, as illustrated in FIG. 15-8. When the box-like form is well aligned put it to one side until the glue is dry.

Fig. 15-8. When all the parts come together for a good fit, check that they are all the right way around, and then glue, nail, and clamp.

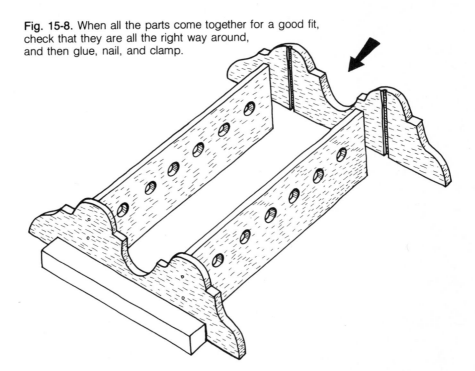

Traditionally, little kitchen pieces of this character were painted—nothing very bright, overshiny, or subtle, just honest earth colors like brick red, brown, and green. Take your chosen, suitably muted, acrylic color and mix it with a little water and dried milk powder to make a creamy paint. Now take the shelf and lay on a couple of well-brushed coats. When the paint has dried to a characteristic and rather beautiful dull sheen, take a scrap of sandpaper and swiftly rub down the shelf at corners and edges to give it a worn-look patina.

- You might redesign the project so that there are say four shelves, or the shelves are longer.

- You might make the shelf as described, and then pin it to a decorative backing board. (See the inspirational designs.)

PROJECT 16

WHITTLING AND PAINTING A
Mr. Punch Puppet Head
IN THE *English Tradition*

Fig. 16-1. A traditional
Mr. Punch head. Note
the characteristic features:
the huge nose, the hooked
chin, and the lascivious smile.

Mr. Punch, short for Punchinello, a type of clown, is the chief character in the traditional puppet show of Punch and Judy. He is usually represented as a grotesque, hook-nosed, hook-jawed, humpbacked man (FIG. 16-1). As to the origins of Mr. Punch, some authorities suggest that he has his roots in old English mummers' plays and that he is the archetypal evil character—a sort of cross between the devil and an anti-Crusader Turkish villain. Others suggest that he has to do with a certain Manducus Dossennus, a hunchbacked ogre with clamping jaws, who was a popular character in ancient Roman farces.

All we know for sure is that, by the seventeenth century, Mr. Punch was a well-established love/hate figure in English puppet shows. By the nineteenth century, Punch-and-Judy shows were very popular in England, so much so that there were many famous showmen who made a good living traveling the land giving puppet performances at fairs and country wakes.

As a character, Punch is a real beauty who spends most of his time beating his wife, killing babies, and fighting with the law. At one time, the making of these puppet heads must have been all part and parcel of the work of the country rustic wood carver cum toy maker.

Materials

A piece of lime wood that measures about 5×5 inches square and 6 inches long
Plasticine modeling paste
A block-and-stick stand (see details)
Acrylic paints, colors to suit

Tools

A coping saw
A hand drill
A 1-inch-diameter drill bit
A couple of knives, say a broad-bladed penknife and a scalpel
A bench and vise
Work-out paper and pencils
A ruler
Fine-point paintbrushes
Various workshop odds and ends like cloths and paint tubs

DESIGN AND TECHNIQUE

Before you start this project, visit a museum, a toy collection, or a puppet theater, and view as many examples of traditional puppets as possible. Study puppets made in the East, and of course all the semi-mass-produced wood-carved puppet heads that were made in the early nineteenth century in German districts like Sonneberg and Nuremberg. Most important of all, have a good look at English wood-carved puppet heads as made in the eighteenth and early nineteenth century (FIG. 16-2).

Fig. 16-2. Inspirational designs

Judy

A friendly Mr. Punch

The policeman

A magistrate

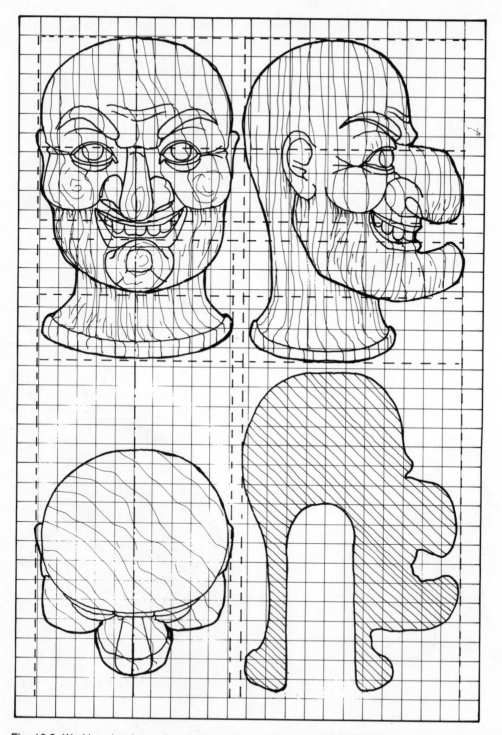

Fig. 16-3. Working drawings—the grid scale is 3 squares to 1 inch. Note how the wood grain runs from neck to crown and how the finger hole is off-center.

When you get to see these carvings, and I must warn you that they are going to need a bit of searching out, have a close-up look and see how the carved profiles and features have all the vigor and humor of some of the early twentieth-century American caricature whittlings. Note the strong, bold lines and the absence of fussy details, and perhaps most important of all, see how the puppets have been designed and worked so that they make a powerful visual impact.

When you have had a look at as many wooden puppet heads as possible, sit down with a work pad and a soft pencil and make a series of study sketches. Make notes as to size and color, measure the size of features like eyes and nose, and generally collect as much information as time and tide allows.

When you are well into the subject, sit down with a block of Plasticine modeling paste—it is best if this can be done in the museum with a couple of good puppets in front of you—and make a full-size maquette or replica model. At this stage don't fuss around with little details, but just aim to capture the overall character.

Setting Out the Design and First Cuts

When you have established through your exploratory work-outs in Plasticine and on paper just how you want your puppet head to be, then make a gridded master drawing—that is a drawing that shows the front view, the side profile, the plan, and the various details (FIG. 16-3).

Take a tracing of the views and pencil-press transfer the traced lines through to the working faces of your block of wood. Make sure that the lines indicate clearly the areas of waste that need to be cut away. Then set out your tools.

Start by up-ending your wood and marking out the position of the finger hole. Noting that the hole needs to be placed off-center, set a depth stop on your drill, secure the block of wood in the vise, and bore out the hole.

Now take the coping saw, and very carefully cut away the waste from the side profile. Clear the waste from the top of the head, from around the brow, from the top of the nose, from between the nose and the chin, and from underneath the jaw (FIG. 16-4).

Whittling the Form

When you have established the beautiful hooked-nosed side profile, then refer to your working drawings and see how, in the front view, the areas of waste occur either side of the top of the head, just below the line of the cheekbones, and at the neck. Pencil in these areas on the front of the profile.

Now take your knife and make stop cuts from the nose around the side of the head and up over the ears; from under the nose, around under the cheekbones to the ears; and from under the jaw to the lower side of the ears (FIG. 16-5). Bearing in mind that these cuts not only mark out the position of the ears, jaw, and so on, but also act as depth guides, cut straight down into the grain to a depth of about ⅛ to ¼ inch. Now hold the block of wood as you might hold a large apple that you are about to peel, and make sloping

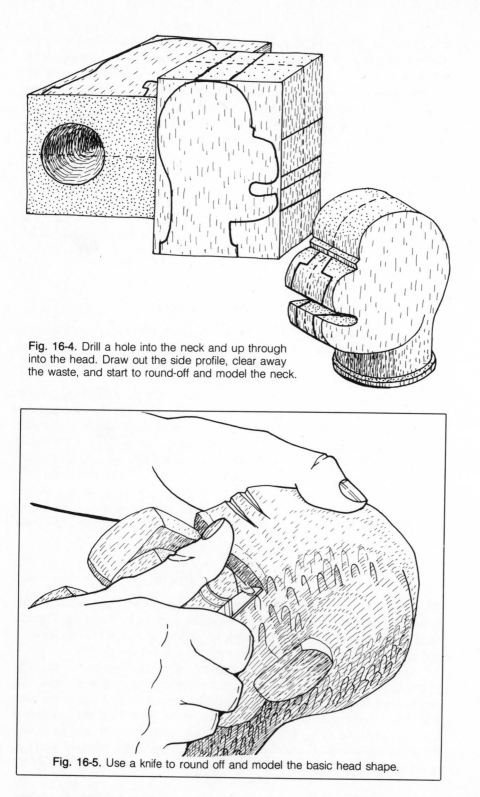

Fig. 16-4. Drill a hole into the neck and up through into the head. Draw out the side profile, clear away the waste, and start to round-off and model the neck.

Fig. 16-5. Use a knife to round off and model the basic head shape.

or angled cuts into the stop cuts. In this way, whittle and shape the round rimmed neck at the underside of the jaw, and the curves and dips that occur at either side of the head.

By variously paring, rounding, and chopping into the stop cuts, you will very soon achieve the steps and roundnesses that go to make up the form (FIG. 16-6). At this stage, don't try to overwork any particular areas; just settle for a form that is made up of a series of steps, slopes, and faceted roundnesses.

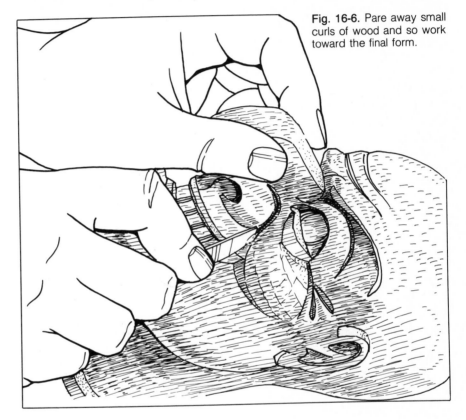

Fig. 16-6. Pare away small curls of wood and so work toward the final form.

Modeling and Detailing

Now, with the wood cradled in one hand and one of your knives held in the other, continue modeling and detailing the head with an increasingly gentle paring action. Don't, in the first instance, attempt to take any particular area or detail to a fine finish. It is much better to work over the form gradually, bringing the whole project closer to completion.

As you work, be prepared to change your knife and/or adjust your approach to suit the job in hand. For example, when you are carving the ears, you might support and steady the work with one hand, while you carve and whittle with the fine-point scalpel held, penlike in the other.

You will, of course, need to continually adjust the angle and the direction of cut so that you don't dig straight down into end grain. It is best if you work across or at an angle to the grain. If you have doubts as to the direction of the grain or how you should be cutting, let the knife and the wood be your guide. That is, if the waste wood curls away and leaves the form looking crisp and smooth, then all is well. On the other hand, if the wood tears up ragged and rough, or the knife keeps juddering and running into the grain, then as likely as not you are approaching the grain from the wrong direction.

As you work, always keep your knives razor sharp and be constantly aware of the changing character of the wood. Finally, when you are within a whisker of finishing, take the sharpest, finest scalpel and work over the whole surface of the wood with a delicate feather-light touch, rounding a detail there, cutting in a sharp edge here, reworking a fine line, and so on.

PAINTING

When you consider the work finished—and this will of course mean different things to different people—clear away all the clutter. Pin up as many color notes, museum illustrations, and magazine photographs as possible. Set out your paints and brushes and mount the finished head on a block-and-stick stand (FIG. 16-7).

Again, exactly what colors you choose to use or how you apply the paint is up to you. Refer to traditional Mr. Punch heads and see how the colors are characteristically bold and strong, and applied to give the strongest possible visual impact. For example, you will need to use plenty of bright, fleshy pinks and florid reds for the cheeks, the lips, the point of the nose, and the chin. The eyes need to be large, dark, and piercing. When you begin painting, start by laying on a white/pink matte base or undercoat, then work up from an all-over flesh pink ground through to the features, and finish with the details around the eyes.

As to how the puppet is put together—Mr. Punch is usually a glove puppet, meaning the head is operated by the puppet master's index finger, while the arms are operated by his thumb and third finger. This being so, the puppet is best built dolllike, with the arms, legs, paunch, and chest being made up from small sewn and stuffed forms that are hung from a basic gloved form. The costume can be gathered round the neck of the wood-carved head (FIG. 16-8). Finally sign and date the back of the head and the job is done.

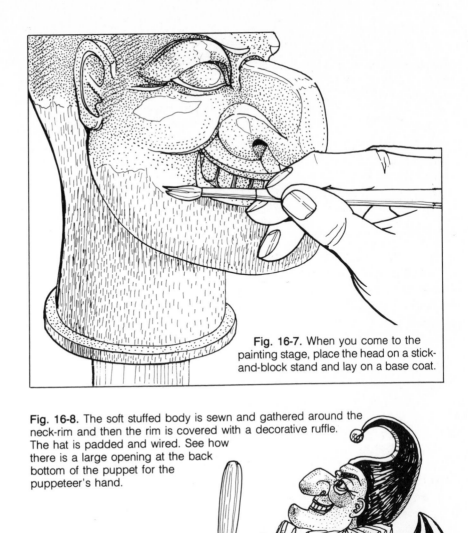

Fig. 16-7. When you come to the painting stage, place the head on a stick-and-block stand and lay on a base coat.

Fig. 16-8. The soft stuffed body is sewn and gathered around the neck-rim and then the rim is covered with a decorative ruffle. The hat is padded and wired. See how there is a large opening at the back bottom of the puppet for the puppeteer's hand.

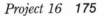

- When you come to making the Plasticine maquette, bear in mind that the features need to be bold and exaggeratedly overlarge—the eyes, nose, cheeks, chin, and mouth must all be positive forms.

- When you are drilling the initial neck hole, make sure that it is placed off-center with the block of wood (see details).

- When you are choosing your materials, make sure that you go for an easily worked wood, like lime.

PROJECT 17

DECORATING *Furniture* IN THE *American Stencil Tradition*

Fig. 17-1. A traditional Hitchcock chair.

In 1826, or thereabouts, a certain Lambert Hitchcock, an established chairmaker, built a factory at Hitchcocksville, Connecticut, now Riverton. It was there, between the years 1826 and 1852, with a work force of about 100 men and women, that he produced vast numbers of his now-famous stencil-decorated chairs (FIG. 17-1). These chairs are characterized by their beautiful hard-edged, gold and bronze, flower- and fruit-inspired, stencil designs (FIG. 17-2).

Fig. 17-2. Detail of the chair-back motif, gold on black.

Of course, there were many other chairmakers who produced similar designs—Jarred Johnson and W.P. Eaton, to name but two—but Hitchcock was so commercially successful that all the stenciled chairs of this period have come to be called *Hitchcock chairs*, or Hitchcock-type chairs. In fact, so great was the demand for his product, it is reckoned that over a 25-year period the factory produced well nigh one-half million chairs. Unfortunately, it has been said of these chairs that, because they are factory made, they cannot truly be described as being within the folk-art tradition. Certainly they were mass produced, and yes they were a conventional factory item inasmuch as they were assembled by a team of workers, but at the same time we now know that Hitchcock chairs not only drew their inspiration directly from Norwegian and German folk crafts, but also in their production they were decorated by primitive artists. A mass-produced factory product maybe, but they were and, since the factory has reopened, they still are stencil decorated in the spirit of the American folk-art tradition (FIG. 17-3).

Fig. 17-3. Inspirational designs—A rather more flamboyant American stenciled motif. Note the eagle, shield, and crossed banners.

A chair or another piece of furniture to stencil
A clear oil-based lacquer or varnish
An oil-based gold paint
A selection of gold and bronze powders (ask for gilder's powders)
Oil-based black paint

Cartridge paper
Tracing paper, work-out paper, pencils
Two sheets of stencil card of a size to suit
A pack of graded sandpapers
A cutting board
A fine-point scalpel and a pack of spare blades
Felt-tip pens
Fine-point and broad paintbrushes
A striping brush
Odds and ends like newspapers, turpentine, and cloths

DESIGN AND TECHNIQUE

Before you start this project, visit a museum of American folk art and get to see a Hitchcock chair. Try to find a chair made about 1840. When you view such a chair, take a good, long look. See how the varnish-covered bronze-powder stencil designs look to be inlaid. Note how the designs are made up from two or more stencils. See also how the chair form has been embellished, picked out, and emphasized with hand-painted gold striping. If necessary, take a magnifying glass to the back-splat stencil decoration, and study how the design has been achieved. Note how the hard-edged fruit and flower forms have been stenciled on a dark ground and then overstenciled with textural details like leaf veins, buds, pips, and flower centers.

The actual stencil techniques were recorded at the time as follows: '' . . . the piece to be decorated is lacquered, then when the lacquer is almost dry, precious metallic powders are dribbled and brushed through the stencil onto the sticky lacquer. Finally the piece is rubbed down and relacquered.'' By lacquering, trickling bronze powders on the lacquer, relacquering, and so on, it is possible to create designs that have visual and physical depth.

When you have studied the museum piece in detail, sit back with the work-out paper and make a series of sketches. Try to break the design down into its separate stencilings.

When you get back to your workshop, have a look at our working drawings (FIG. 17-4), and see how this particular design relates to a two-stencil motif. Note also how the two stencil plates need to be *registered*, or aligned, by matching up stencil-plate holes. Once you have taken note of all the design and technique

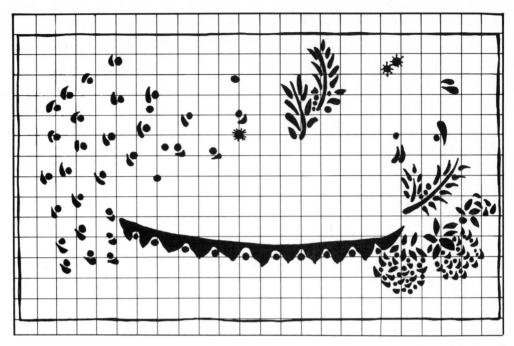

Fig. 17-4. Working drawings—scale to suit. *(top)* the ''details'' stencil plate; *(below)* the ''main areas'' plate. Note that all black areas are holes or design windows.

implications and you have a fair understanding of just how the stencil technique works, take the layout pad and either copy our design directly, or make modifications. Finally, make a master design, and break it down into two parts: the main *form* stencil, meaning the shape of the fruit, leaves, and flowers; and the *details* stencil, meaning the leaf veins and the highlights.

Making the Stencil Plates

When you have drawn up the master design, take the tracing paper and a soft pencil and make two tracings: a tracing of the main forms and a tracing of the details. When you have made the two tracings, lay one on top of the other and make sure that they come together to make the total design. Mark in the registration holes (FIG. 17-5). Then, take a hard pencil and pencil-press transfer the traced lines through to the working face of the stencil card.

Working on a dense-surfaced cutting board, either a sheet of hardboard, or better still a piece of plate glass, start to cut out the windows of the design. Using a short-bladed fine-point scalpel, draw the knife toward you with one hand, and guide, maneuver, and turn the card with the other. Try to keep the card moving so the scalpel blade is always presented with the line of next cut. Aim to cut the card so all the windows are smooth edged, clean, and nicely formed.

When you have cut and worked the main stencil plate, check that it relates to the second plate tracing—the tracing of the details—then cut and work the second plate in like manner. Take special care with the second plate. Make several checks to make sure the details are correctly aligned. If you have any doubts, use the felt-tip pens and the work-out paper and do a trial stenciling. If necessary, adjust one or other of the stencil plates for a better fit.

Once you have made two well-cut, correctly aligned plates and you have established the registration holes, then clear the work surface of all clutter, pin up your inspirational material, and set out your tools and materials so that everything is comfortably at hand.

Laying the Ground

Take your piece to be decorated well away from your working area, and rub it down with the graded sandpapers until it is completely smooth (FIG. 17-6). Work the sandpapers from medium-rough to super-fine, and aim to leave the surface smooth, sound, and free from dust and debris. If necessary, wipe the chair down with a turpentine-dampened cloth. This done, take your base paint—it is best to go for black or a subtle dark color like dull red or deep blue—make sure that the paint is well mixed and free from bits, then lay on a single, well-brushed thin coat. When the paint is dry, take the finest sandpaper and cut back ground with a few swift, delicate strokes. NOTE: it is a good idea to keep some lines to prepare a trial piece; that is, prepare and paint a piece of scrap wood.

When the paint is completely dry, take the chair back into the workshop, and set it out on the work surface so that the area to be decorated is horizontal and at a good height. Finally, make sure that the windows are closed and your working area is as dust free as possible. Then take a soft, flat brush and lay a thin coat of lacquer on the areas that are to be decorated.

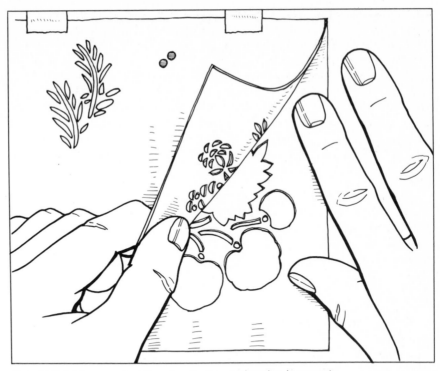

Fig. 17-5. Make sure that the stencil plate registration is correct.

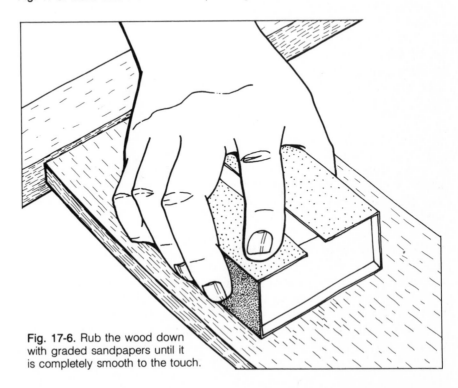

Fig. 17-6. Rub the wood down with graded sandpapers until it is completely smooth to the touch.

Dusting the Bronze Powders

When the lacquer or varnish is still sticky, but dry enough for you to touch without your fingers sticking, then you can work the first stencil. Place and press the first stencil plate in position, then take up a little bronze powder in a fold of paper and carefully dribble it around one of the stencil plate windows (FIG. 17-7). Working with a fine, soft brush or a fingertip and a piece of velvet, grade the bronze powder from side to center. Because there is really no going back once you have started, be cautious and work the stencil windows little by little. Continue to work the various windows of the design, until you gradually build up the density of the bronze powder shading from edge to center.

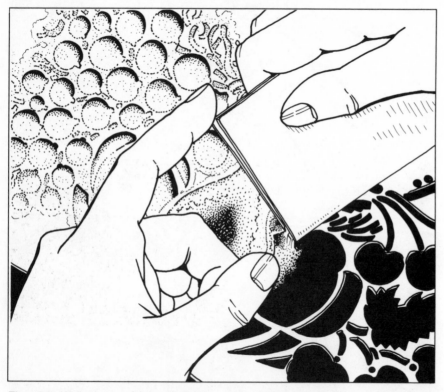

Fig. 17-7. While the varnish is still slightly sticky, dribble the gold powder through the stencil windows. Use a brush or fingertip to grade the powder from side to center.

When you consider the stencil windows well dusted, carefully gather all the excess powder and very gently peel up the stencil plate. If by chance you spill a little bronze powder, or some of it creeps under the stencil plate, either wipe it up with a varnish-soaked fluff-free cloth, or better still, wait for the varnish to dry and then dab out your mistakes with a little of the ground paint.

When the varnish or lacquer is completely dry, and this will probably be after about 48 hours, wipe the stenciled area over with a damp cloth, just to make sure that all the excess powder has been removed, then start the second stenciling. Now the second printing is more or less the same as the first; that is to say, you apply the varnish, wait for it to dry out, position the stencil plate, and so on. The registration holes of the second plate must be perfectly aligned with the first print, and because the windows in the second plate are smaller, the powder needs to be applied with greater care. To this end, it might be helpful to use a fine-point or stencil brush when you are trying to powder a very small stencil window (FIG. 17-8). Apply the powder thoroughly, but at the same time be careful that you don't force it under the edge of the stencil plate.

Fig. 17-8. When you come to stenciling the small details, use a fine brush to push the gold powder through the stencil plate holes.

When you have worked the second stencil, or perhaps the third or fourth if you are doing a really ambitious design, wait for 48 hours for the varnish to dry, then clean up or dab out any bronze powder faults, and lay on another coat of varnish. This time, however, varnish the whole chair.

When the varnish is completely dry, rub down swiftly with the finest sandpaper and then apply a last thin coat. Finally, make sure that the chair is free from dribbles and runs, then put it to one side to dry.

STRIPING AND FINISHING

When the final coat of varnish/lacquer is dry, clear the work surface of all clutter and establish in your own mind just where the striping ought to be. Then set out the striping brush, the turpentine, the gold paint, and the various tubs and cloths. Stir and mix the gold paint, pour a little into a tub, and then add a few drops of varnish. Stir well, then dip the striping brush into the mixture and have a trial run on your scrap of wood.

Hold the brush between your thumb and index finger. Using your small finger as a gauge or guide, run the line around the stenciled design, as illustrated in FIG. 17-9. There are no tricks, other than that the brush needs to be pulled toward you; the gold paint and varnish need to be well mixed; and you must work with a steady, confident hand. Practice makes perfect.

When the gold striping is dry, swiftly lay on another coat of varnish and the job is done.

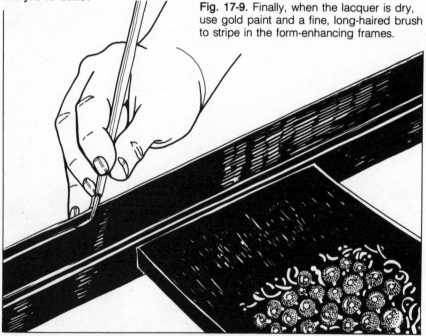

Fig. 17-9. Finally, when the lacquer is dry, use gold paint and a fine, long-haired brush to stripe in the form-enhancing frames.

• When varnishing, always work in a dust-free, dry, still environment. It is best if the temperature is about 70° F and the day is dry. If you try varnishing on a wet or humid day, the varnish might refuse to dry or go bloomy or cloudy.

• Always keep a brush especially for varnishing. Never dip your brush in the varnish can; always pour a little varnish into a tub.

• This project must not be rushed. If you revarnish before the ground varnish or paint is dry or dust the bronze powder when the varnish is too sticky, you will have problems.

PROJECT 18

MAKING AND DECORATING A
Salt Box
IN THE
American Fractur Tradition

Fig. 18-1. A traditional salt box with fracture lettering, hinged lid, and characteristic motifs.

Not so long ago, wooden salt boxes were a common item in most households (FIG. 18-1). Made variously of oak, pine, sycamore, or maple, they usually were to be found hanging on the wall within easy reach of the cooking range and the fireplace.

Such boxes were made, more often than not, by a local craftsman or the man of the house. Consequently they tended to be very simple in structure and form: a shaped and fretted backing plate, a hand-sized salt compartment built out from the backing plate, a pivoted lid, and, because of the corrosive qualities of salt on metal, the whole thing held together with wooden pins. As for design, decorative styles, and methods of working, these were many and varied. Boxes were chip carved, relief carved, poker worked, inlaid, painted, and so on.

Because salt boxes were homely and unpretentious, their form and style usually reflected the ordinary decorative traditions of the area and period in which they were made. One such salt box type was that decorated in the American folk *fracktur-schriften* or fractur tradition. Originally a style of European calligraphy and later a printer's typeface, fractur was taken to America by the Pennsylvania Dutch. In its Old-World form, fractur related to illuminated and decorated lettering. In Germany and Switzerland, it was used by schoolmasters, the clergy, and the legal profession when they were drawing up special documents, such as marriage papers, birth certificates, and property titles.

What makes American fractur so interesting is not the fact that it survived and continued to be used well into the twentieth century—almost 200 years after it had died out in Europe—but rather that in its stimulating New World setting, the craft developed and blossomed into a uniquely beautiful decorative art in its own right. As this project bears out, one such remarkable fractur development was that of decorating boxes, chests, and furniture with brilliantly painted lettering and motifs. The decorative style that has now come to be called "folk American fractur" is characterized by the use of brilliant colors, bold black-edged patterns, exciting pattern-filled frames and borders, Gothic letterforms, charming little figures, and a great deal of traditional design and motif symbolism. For example, salt boxes were decorated with religious three-petal Trinity tulips, love hearts, initial, dates, eagles, and clocks (FIG. 18-2). See also Project 9.

Materials

About 5 board feet of prepared 6-x-½-inch pine, oak, or
sycamore (meaning a piece of prepared wood, 60 inches long,
6 inches wide, and ½ inch thick)
A small quantity of PVA glue
Acrylic paints, color to suit
A tin of boat varnish

Tools

A bench vise
A set of clamps
A small hammer
A straight saw   (. . . continued)

Fig. 18-2. Inspirational designs.

A coping saw
A sharp clasp knife
A square
A ruler
A compass
A small hand drill with a $\frac{3}{16}$-inch bit
graded sandpapers
A selection of broad and fine-point brushes
Tracing paper, work-out paper
Cloths and paint-mixing tubs

DESIGN AND TECHNIQUE

Before you start this project, take a trip to a museum of American folk art, and view examples of early nineteenth century fractur work. See how the designs are usually symmetrically orgainized, and note how the patterns and motifs are picked out with vigorous, bold, black-line edging. See also the beautiful Gothic-style letterforms. Generally consider how the designs, patterns, and motifs have been worked in a generous, direct, primitive style.

Make a set of pen and ink sketches. In so doing, try to capture some of the childlike innocence of the originals. Study also our inspirational designs.

This done, have a look at our working drawings (FIG. 18-3); take note of form, structure, and sizes; then design your own salt box. Once you have achieved what you consider to be a well thought out box design, then draw the various elevations out to size and finalize details and fixings.

Now trace off the elevations—meaning the top, front, and sides of the box—have yet another look at our inspirational patterns and motifs, then work out your own decorations accordingly. Take note of your museum work-out sketches, and draw up your own paint list (FIG. 18-4). Go for traditional colors like black, sepia, brick red, deep blue, mustard yellow, and light leaf green. Finally, once you have drawn up your own structure and decoration designs or modified ours, then take a good tracing.

Setting Out the Wood and First Cuts

Once you get your length of prepared 6-x-½-inch wood back to the workshop, make sure that it is free from splits and dead knots. Now have a look at the working drawing grid. With a pencil, ruler, and square, mark off the six lengths that go to make up the salt box: the back plate, the front, the two sides, the lid, and the base. NOTE: if you do need to use wood that is less than perfect, try to organize the setting out so that the faults occur on the inside of the box or on the underside of the base.

Have a last check, just to make doubly sure that the setting out is correct, then take the straight saw and cut the board down. Take the six short lengths of wood and label them "side," "front," and so on. It is also a good idea at this stage to establish and label the working face of the various box sides.

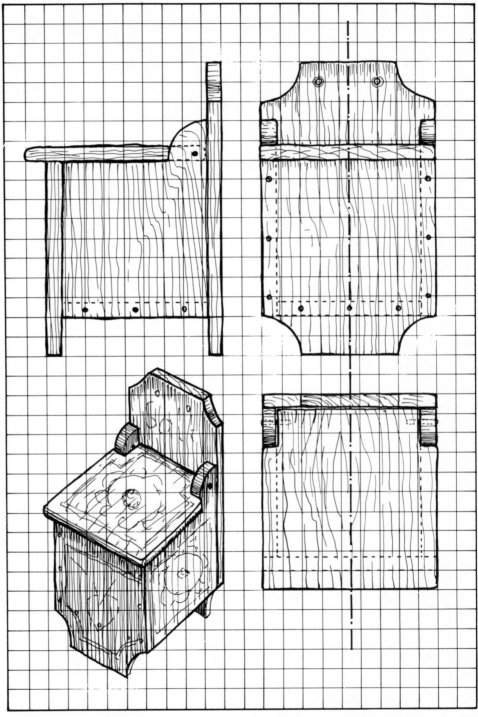

Fig. 18-3. Working drawings—the grid scale is about 3 squares to 2 inches. Note how the lid needs to be peg pivoted and peg fixed to avoid problems with metal-salt corrosion.

Fig. 18-4. Painting grid. Note how all the colors are edged with a black line.

Shaping

Look at the working drawings and see how, although the design is relatively uncomplicated, all six box sides do need to be cut, adjusted, and shaped. So, one piece at a time and working with the square, ruler, and compass, mark out the four back-plate corner curves, the two front-plate corner curves, and the two side-plate hinge curves. To do so, set the compass radius at about 1⅜ inches, and strike off the quarter-circle arcs, as illustrated.

Secure the marked out wood in the vise, then with the coping saw cut away the various curve-profiled waste pieces. Working the wood with the coping saw is pretty straightforward, as long as you steady the wood with one hand and guide and maneuver the saw with the other. Keep the saw blade at right angles to the working face of the wood. When you have cut away all the waste, take the graded sandpapers and remove all the ragged edges and burrs.

Putting Together

After the wood has been swiftly rubbed down, then clear away the bench clutter and start putting the box together. Have a look at the working drawings and see how the box sides have been drilled, glued, and pinned with knife-cut dowels.

Sandwich the base between the two sides, as illustrated in FIG. 18-5, and clamp. Then take the hand drill and work the ³⁄₁₆-inch dowel holes. See how there are three holes per edge, and bore the holes to a depth of about ⅞ inch. Now, knife-cut a dozen or so tight-fit dowels—it is best if they are about 1 inch long, octagonal in section, and slightly pointed.

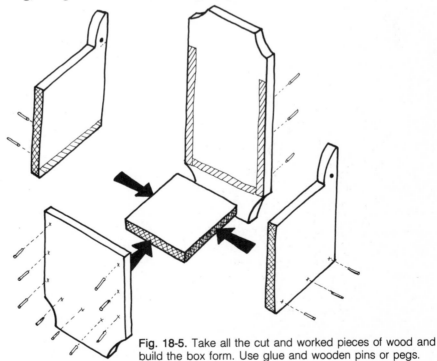

Fig. 18-5. Take all the cut and worked pieces of wood and build the box form. Use glue and wooden pins or pegs.

When you have cut the wooden dowels, remove the clamps, glue the edges, and then fix the sides to the base with the dowel pins. Now locate, drill, glue, and pin the other sides of the box in a like manner. Check that the box sides are square, then clamp, and put the assembly to one side until the glue has set.

While the glue is drying, take the lid piece, mark it out so that it fits the box, then cut away the two corner hinge notches. Check for a good fit, then take the rasp and the graded sandpapers, and shape and rub down all the sides and angles (FIG. 18-6). Aim for edges that are round-nosed in section.

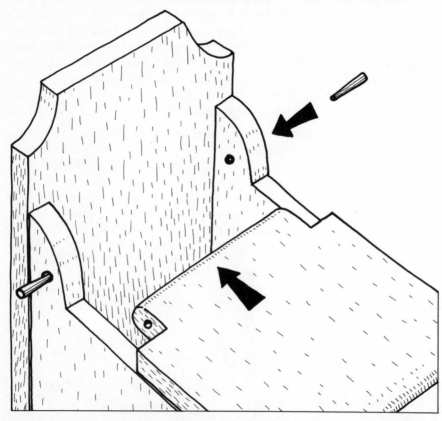

Fig. 18-6. Round the front and back edges of the lid flap, slide it into place, and hold it in place with wooden pivot pins.

When the glue is dry, trim and fit the lid, and drill and pin the hinge pivot holes. Now take two dowel pins, cut them to a slight taper, then dab a little glue in the pivot holes and bang the pins home. Aim for a lid that is a nice, easy, loose fit.

When the glue is dry, swing the lid open a few times, and trim the curve of the hinge bracket to a good finish. Finally, take the graded sandpapers and go over the whole box, rubbing down to a good, smooth, worn-look finish. All corners, edges, and profiles should be rounded.

PAINTING: Preparing the Ground and Lining In

When the box has been rubbed down well, select your acrylic ground color, make sure that the box is free from dust, then lay on a couple of well-brushed coats. When the paint is dry, take tracings from the master design and pencil-press transfer the traced lines through to the various faces of the box. Make sure that the transferred lines are well established, maybe go over them with a soft pencil. If necessary, adjust and modify the design to fit additions like dates and names.

When you have done this, take a fine-point brush and the black paint, and carefully line-in all the motifs and the patterns that go to make up the design (FIG. 18-7). Try to keep the black lines smooth, even, and unbroken. Make sure that each and every outline is well considered and cleanly established. From time to time, stand back from your work and consider the design as a whole. If necessary, adjust and modify the motifs and patterns as you go along. NOTE: paint a piece of scrap wood in like manner.

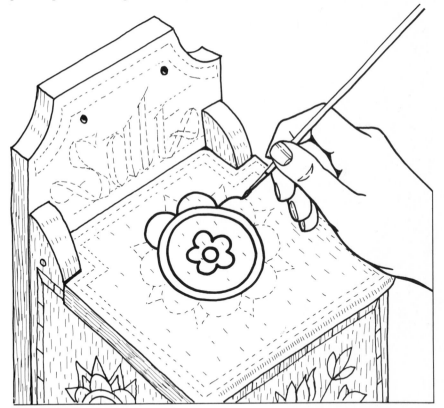

Fig. 18-7. Pencil-press transfer the lines of the design and then go over the drawn lines with black paint and a fine-point brush.

Blocking in the Color and Finishing

When you have set-in the whole smooth-curved black line design, have another look at your inspirational color sketches and notes, then arrange your colors and brushes so that they are all close at hand.

Start by having a trial run on the scrap of wood—the piece that you have ground painted and black lined. When you have achieved a well-balanced color arrangement, take your chosen paints, mix them to a good consistency, and have another tryout on the scrap of wood. Aim to achieve a swift, fluid, loose-wristed action.

This done, start blocking in the colors (FIG. 18-8). Paint the heart, the tulip, the large abstracted flower motifs, the edge borders, the lettering, and so on, until all the design windows have been blocked in. When you feel that the design is finished, clean your brushes.

Fig. 18-8. Finally, block-in the black-edged design areas with the colors of your choice.

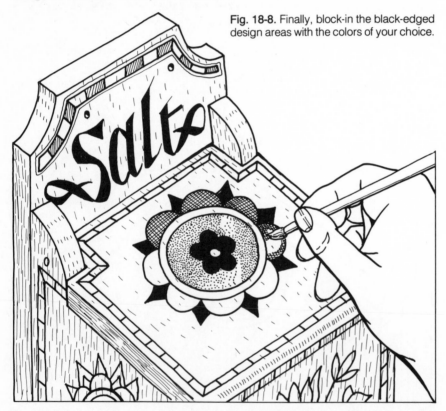

When the paint has had time to dry, take the finest sandpaper and swiftly cut through the paint at corners and edges to give a beautiful worn effect. Finally wipe the box over with a damp cloth, just to make sure that it is free from dust, then lay on a couple of coats of yacht varnish.

- This project uses wooden pins because of the corrosive qualities of salt on metal. If you are going to modify the project and make, say a box for flour, bread, tea, or some such, then there is no reason at all why you shouldn't put the box together with brass pins or oval nails.

- We have chosen to use acrylic paints because they have a very fast drying time—so fast that the colors can touch each other without bleeding. You might adjust the project and use milk paints, household gloss paints, artist colors, or modeler's enamels. (See the *Workshop Data* section.)

19

MAKING AND PAINTING
Roundels
IN THE
English Elizabethan Tradition

Fig. 19-1. A traditional roundel with gilded and painted designs and space for a poesy.

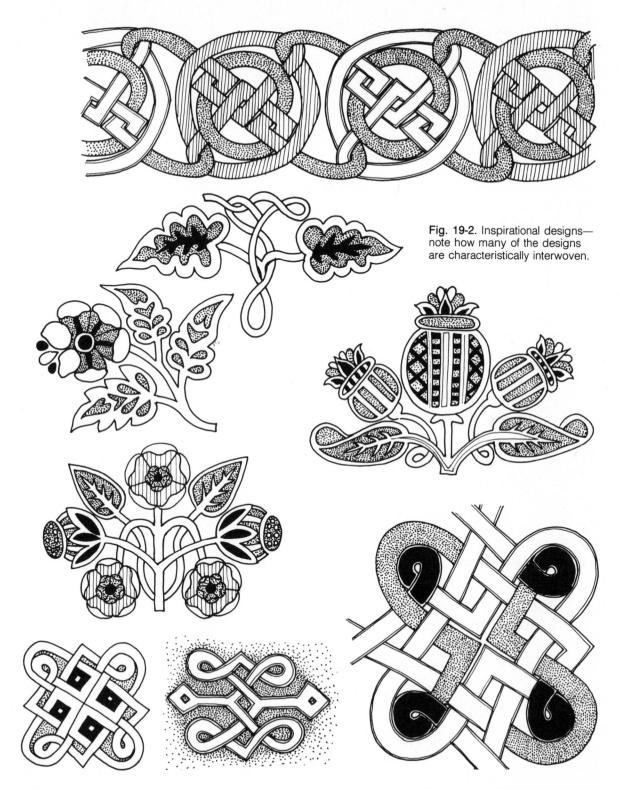

Fig. 19-2. Inspirational designs—note how many of the designs are characteristically interwoven.

Roundels, as made in the time of Queen Elizabeth (about 1550), are rather delicate circular wooden trenchers. Between 5 to 6 inches in diameter, about ¼ inch thick, and made of sycamore or beech, roundels of this type, date, and character are usually plain on one side and painted and gilded with designs, motifs, patterns, and *poesies* on the other (FIG. 19-1).

What are poesies? Well the answer is straightforward enough. The beautiful archaic word *poesy* simply means "poetry." In the context of this project, a poesy is a few lines of verse or a little song that is worked in ornamental lettering on the decorative side of the roundel.

In use, roundels were set out on the table after the main course, and then used for the more delicate confettes or conceits; that is to say, for cheese, marzipans, and sugar plums. As to why they were decorated with poetry—at the end of the meal, when the guests had finished, the roundels were turned over so that the poesies were face up, and then each of the guests entertained the company by singing the verse, or roundelay. In George Puttenham's book *The Art of English Poesie,* written in 1589, he says of roundels, " . . . there be also epigrames . . . we call them poesies and do paint them now dayes upon the backside of our fruit trenchers . . . "

In many ways, roundels and roundelays have come to characterize the whole rather romantic Elizabethan period. Banquets, lute music, knot gardens, poesies, roundels, and love ballards—they are all beautifully evocative. Elizabethan roundels are nearly always decorated with delicate, interwoven strapwork, painted flowers, and geometrical borders; picked out in brilliant colors, such as red, blue, green, yellow, silver and gold; painted on a dark ground; and protected with a thick golden varnish.

Materials

Six 6-inch-diameter, ¼-inch-thick disks of beech, sycamore, or lime
A set of colored crayon pencils
A selection of best quality modeler's oil paints, colors to include red, black, blue, yellow, silver, and gold
A golden varnish to suit the make and type of paint

Tools

Work-out paper, soft and hard pencils, tracing paper
A pack of graded sandpapers
Masking tape
A compass
A measure
An electric wood-burning tool/pen
A selection of fine-point brushes
A broad, flat varnish brush
A few throwaway mixing tubs, turpentine, cleaning cloths

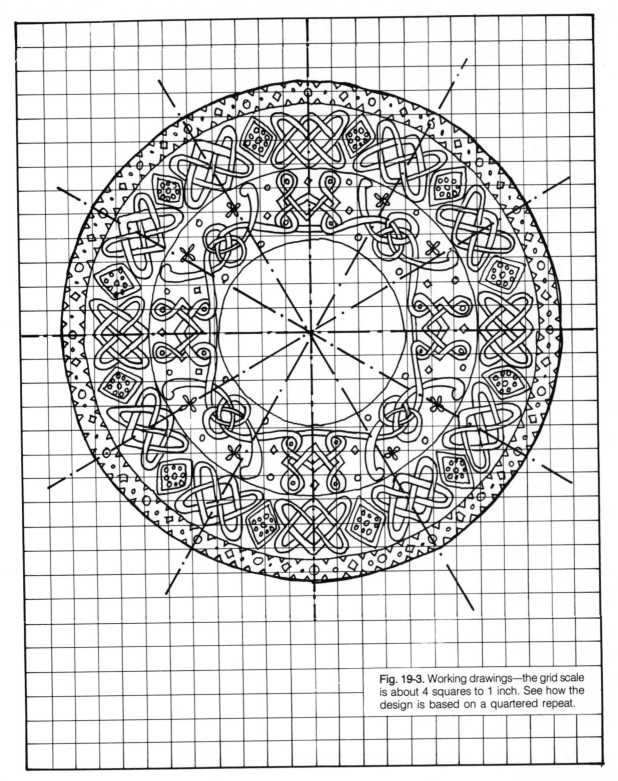

Fig. 19-3. Working drawings—the grid scale is about 4 squares to 1 inch. See how the design is based on a quartered repeat.

DESIGN AND TECHNIQUE

Start this project by having a look at our inspirational patterns and motifs (FIG. 19-2), and our working drawings (FIG. 19-3). See how the designs are characteristically black-lined, interwoven, bold, and altogether strong and vigorous.

This done, take a trip to a museum and see furnishing, fabrics, and wood carvings of the Tudor and Elizabethan periods. Concentrate your efforts on miniatures, embroideries, and jewelry. If possible, use a magnifying glass to study the fine details.

Using a compass and colored pencil crayons, make a series of full-size colored roundel designs. That is to say, draw out half a dozen or so 6-inch-diameter circles, set out borders and bands within the circles, and also break the circles down into quarters and eighths.

When you get back to your working area, pin up your inspirational material, your drawings, museum guides, postcards, magazine clips, etc., then settle down to drawing out a master design. You might decide to go for, say, six slightly different roundel designs, a set of linked motifs that are blocked in with different colors, or whatever. No matter, as long as the overall design effect is of a close, delicate, intricate, involved, intertwined, and convoluted floral pattern.

Now have a look at our working drawings and see how we have modified the traditional technique and set out the black-line structure with a wood-burning pen. It might be as well at this stage, especially if you are a beginner, to have a try-out with such a pen. Practice on a scrap of wood until you are happy with the technique.

If necessary, adjust your designs and motifs. You might go for larger roundels, a broader design, and so on. When you have achieved what you consider is a fair design, select a couple of lines of verse, a saying, a funny ditty, a family name or joke, and work it into the center of your roundel.

Finally, take a fine brush and your selection of paints and block in your practice designs. See how the little black-edged areas of color look to be precious, delicate, and bejeweled. NOTE: if you are unhappy with the wood-burning pen, or you would prefer to use pen and ink or a brush, then reshape the project to suit your needs.

Setting Out the Design

Once you have considered all the possible variations and modifications of the project and have taken into account all the tool and technique implications, then you take your disks of wood and bring them to a good finish. Work through the pack of graded sandpapers, from medium-rough to super-fine, rubbing down to a finish that is as near silky smooth to the touch as possible. Pay particular attention to the face that is to be decorated and the end-grain edges.

Now, take a tracing of your master design. This done, secure the tracing with tabs of masking tape, then pencil-press transfer the traced lines through to the working face of your wood (FIG. 19-4). Use a hard pencil, and systematically work the tracing. When you are sure that all the lines have been transferred, remove the tracing paper, and go over the transferred lines with a pencil.

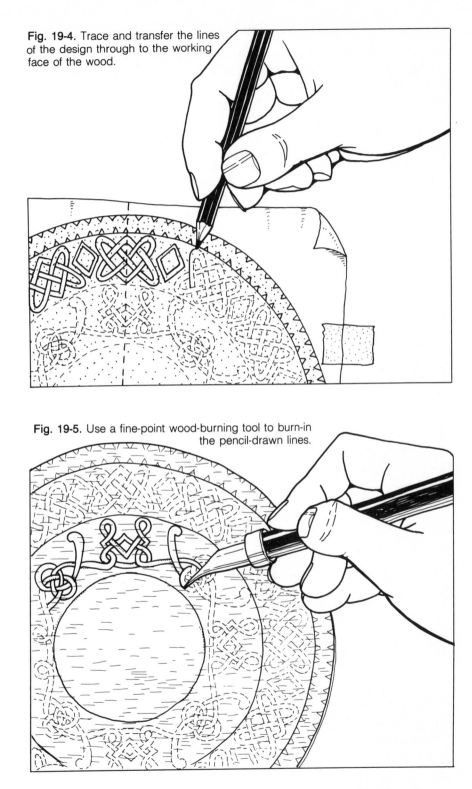

Fig. 19-4. Trace and transfer the lines of the design through to the working face of the wood.

Fig. 19-5. Use a fine-point wood-burning tool to burn-in the pencil-drawn lines.

Setting in the Design with the Wood-Burning Pen

When you have finalized and established the design, then take your wood-burning pen, select and fit the finest point. Switch on the power, allow it to heat up to a dullish red heat, and then start to work (FIG. 19-5).

As you burn in the lines of the design, work with a steady hand. Aim to achieve lines that are smooth flowing and even. Bear in mind, as you are working, not to press too hard, but rather to turn up the heat, and to work with a light touch. Try to keep the pen on the move and to draw with a sensitive stroking action. Above all, don't press so hard that you break or bend the pen, nor so slowly that the tip of the pen flares up and leaves a deep blemish.

What else to say except that practice makes perfect! If you do make a mistake and overrun one of your guidelines, then don't panic, just modify the pattern to take the error into account.

Blocking in the Color

When you have burnt in the design with the wood-burning pen, then comes the pleasuresome task of blocking in the color. Having first established the colors on your master design, take your selected oil paints and stir and mix them until they are smooth, creamy, and not runny. Then clear the work surface of clutter.

Now take up a little color on your finest brush and start the blocking in (FIG. 19-6). Don't be in a rush to finish or overload your brush; just work at a steady pace, blocking in the various colors. So you might fill in all the red areas, then all the blue, and so on. If the colors are well mixed, as described, and if the lines of the design have been evenly burnt in, then the color blocks will each become, as it were, a small, self-contained pool.

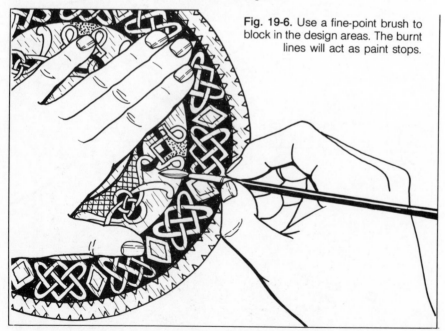

Fig. 19-6. Use a fine-point brush to block in the design areas. The burnt lines will act as paint stops.

We favor limiting colors to the primary range and blocking in so that it looks as if small details and borders are set off against a strong, dark ground. However, it is always wise to follow your own color and design inclinations.

Continue blocking in all the areas that go to make up the total design. It is also a good idea at this stage to lay on a ground color for the letters. So if you want the letters to be, for example, in black, then it is best to lay on a light base color—say white or yellow.

Lettering

When all the colors are dry—and this might take anything from a day to a week, depending on your choice of paints—then comes the tricky business of the lettering. Now brush-worked lettering is difficult, but only inasmuch as the paint needs to be smooth, you must use a fine-point brush, and the letter and word spacing must be carefully considered. Don't think, if you are a beginner, that you can work it all out by eye, and just start at one end of the line and hope to finish up just right at the other end. It hardly ever works out like that. Our advice is to work the letterspacing line by line on tracing paper, and then to pencil-press transfer. Certainly this is a tedious, long drawn out process, but it is well worth the extra effort.

When you have established the position of the lettering, then mix your paint slightly thinner than usual, and then line-in the letters with direct, steady-wristed strokes (FIG. 19-7). As you are working, try to keep wiping the brush to a fine point. If you make a mistake, then be ready with a scrap of cloth and the turpentine. Finally, check that your spelling is correct, and then put the roundel to one side until the paint is dry.

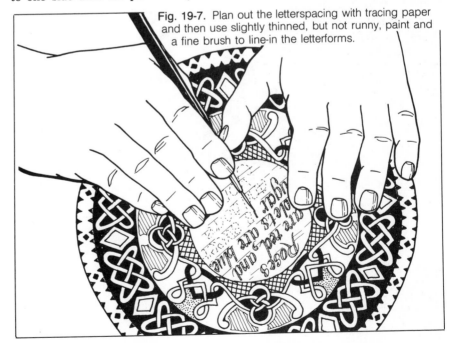

Fig. 19-7. Plan out the letterspacing with tracing paper and then use slightly thinned, but not runny, paint and a fine brush to line-in the letterforms.

A Touch of Gold and Finishing

Clear the working area and set out the roundels, the gold and/or silver paint, the varnish, a fine brush, and a broad, flat brush. First stand back from your work and establish clearly in your mind's eye just how and where you want the gold and silver embellishments to be. For example, do you want to really go to town and pick out the whole design in gold, or are you just going to pick out the center of flowers and maybe the roundel edge? These points need to be well considered before you start.

Again, when you are using the gold and silver paint, don't heap it on, but rather, if it is too thin, lay it on in several coats (FIG. 19-8). Finally, leave the paint to thoroughly dry out, then lay on a couple of coats of well-brushed varnish.

Fig. 19-8. Finally, use good-quality gold and silver paint, and pick out the design.

- When you are choosing your roundel blanks, it is best to go for a close-grained firm wood like sycamore or beech. Avoid knotty, loose-grained, resinous wood.

- It is best to buy thin ready-cut blanks, but if you do want to cut out your own disks, use a coping saw (see other projects).

- If you want to speed up the project, then use acrylic paints rather than oils.

- You might, if you so wish, sandwich the lettering and the gold and silver embellishments between layers of varnish. That is to say, lay on one coat of varnish, let it dry, paint in the lettering, and then lay on the other coat.

- If you are using a wood-burning pen, keep it away from finger-nosey children. The pens do get red hot. They can be very dangerous. Warning! Keep the pen away from inflammable plastics, paints, turpentine, and such.

20

MAKING A

Fretwork and Chip-Carved Distaff

IN THE

English and American Folk Tradition

Fig. 20-1. A traditional pierced and chip-carved distaff. Note how the run of the grain is worked so that fragile, short-grain areas are kept to a minimum.

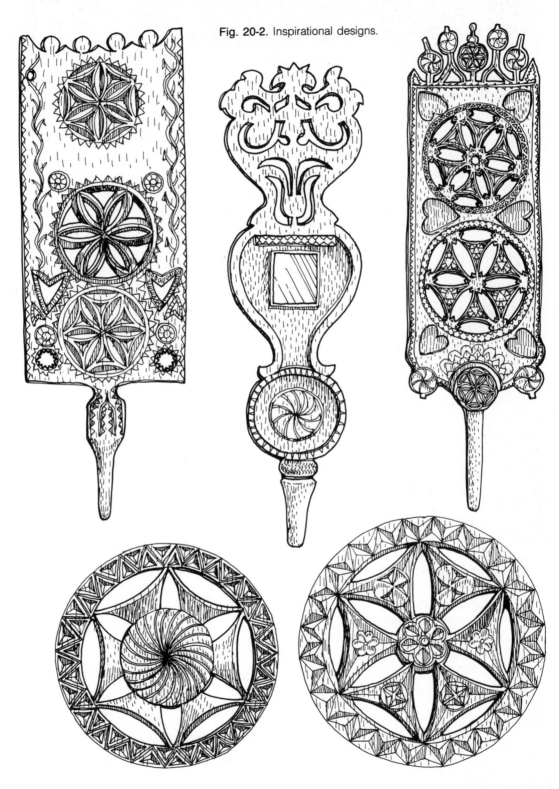

Fig. 20-2. Inspirational designs.

The dictionary describes a *distaff* as a cleft stick on which wool or carded cotton is wound for spinning. It also goes on to compare the term *distaff side,* meaning the female side of the family and the emblem of womanhood, with the term *spear side,* meaning the male side of the family and the emblem of manhood. In most instances the carved distaff is much more than just a craft tool. It is a symbol of feminine status.

Of course this explanation gives some meaning to the fact that distaffs are so amazingly, impractically ornate. They aren't meant to be used as tools, but rather they are ritual display objects that have to do with love tokens, courtship customs, and marriage (FIG. 20-1). Because spinning was usually done by young girls of marriageable age, *spinsters,* then for a girl to receive a carved distaff from, say, the boy next door was particularly significant and meaningful. When a young lad fell in love, he would set to work and carve, as likely as not, a distaff. If the girl of his dreams accepted his present, then it was a sign that he could formally approach her.

The knife-carved twists and turns and the amazing complexity of some of the carved distaffs are a result, not so much of the carver's skill and his love of carving, but rather to the universal keenness of amorous young lads to impress their girls. So it was in English, American, and European folk societies that, long after spinning had ceased to be an important domestic chore, the custom of carving distaffs continued.

Materials

A piece of ¼-inch-thick wood that measures about 6 inches wide and 18 inches long
Beeswax polish

Tools

A workbench
A fretwork sawing board
A fretsaw
A couple of packs of spare saw blades
A sketch pad
Pencils
A compass/dividers
A ruler
A fine-point scalpel
A fine-point penknife
A hand drill with a ⅛-inch-diameter drill bit
Tracing paper
Masking tape

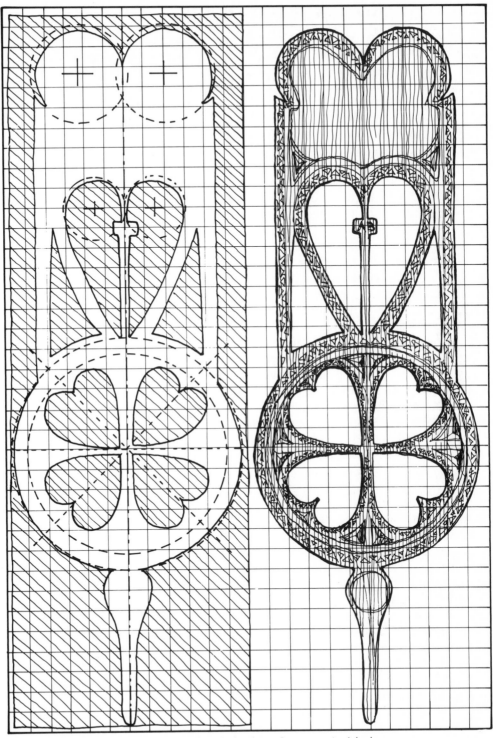

Fig. 20-3. Working drawings—the grid scale is about 2 squares to 1 inch.

DESIGN AND TECHNIQUE

Before you start this project, have a long look at the various inspirational designs (FIG. 20-2) and working drawings (FIG. 20-3), then visit a folk museum and view examples of carved love tokens that were made in England, Europe, and America before c. 1850. Of course, look at the full range of love tokens, like love spoons, mangle boards, stay busks, breadboards, and all the other lover's-type carvings, but concentrate your attention on the distaffs.

When you get a close look at these intricate works of art, make a series of measured drawings and exploratory sketches. See how the designs relate to compass-drawn circles, arcs, quartered circles, and hex circles. Note also how, in the main, the paddlelike forms are pierced and fretted, and then surface-decorated with all manner of chip-carved designs—love hearts; flowers; ancient motifs like crosses, roosters, and the tree of life; and of course dates, initials, and secret signs. Note how characteristically most of the designs are symmetrical.

As for the details of the chip-carved patterns and motifs, take a magnifying glass, and see how the small chip-carved pockets are worked from little single-angled triangular cuts, while the other, larger and more complex pockets are made up from three of the smaller three-facet cuts.

When you have taken note of all the traditional designs, types, and motifs, have another look at the project drawing, and then, in the light of your studies, either copy our designs directly, or change and adapt them to suit your own design inclinations. Of course, if you do want to make a love token, then there's no reason why you shouldn't use the techniques that we describe, but go on to change and update the project and carve say a frame for a photograph, a delicate mount for a work box, or some such.

Finally, when you have decided just how you want your carving to be, draw up a master design, establish a centerline, and take a tracing.

Setting Out the Design

When you have taken a good tracing, pin your master design up near your working area, set out your tools, and spend time making sure that your piece of wood is straight grained and free from splits, dead knots, and stains. Bear in mind that with a project of this intricate character—a project that leaves delicate ''bridges'' of fragile short grain—it is particularly important that the wood be as flawless as possible.

If you are able to choose between various pieces of wood, then take your tracing and see which piece fits best the lines of your chosen design. Then if your wood has a blemish, it might be possible to arrange the design or make small adjustments so that the flaw comes within the waste.

This done, take your tracing and pencil-press transfer the lines of the design through to the working face of the wood.

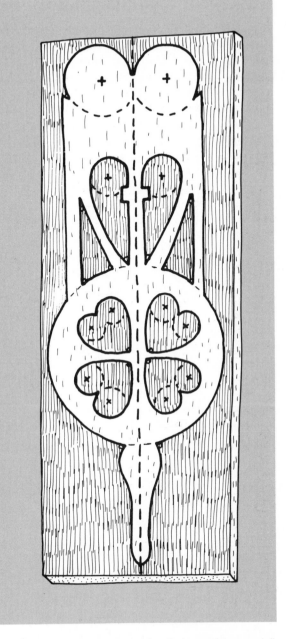

Fig. 20-4. Transfer the lines of the design and then pencil in the areas that need to be cut away and wasted.

Fretting Out the Design

When you have drawn in the lines of the design, cross-hatch the areas of waste—meaning the various edges and "windows" that need to be cut away (FIG. 20-4). Now take the hand drill and the ⅛-inch bit and bore pilot holes through all windows and at tight angle points.

This done, clamp the Vee cutting board to the workbench so that the V hangs well over the edge of the bench, and then start fretting out the design. Position the wood so that the area you want to waste is over the V, and then set to work (FIG. 20-5). Make sure that the teeth of the saw are facing downward and cut on the downward stroke.

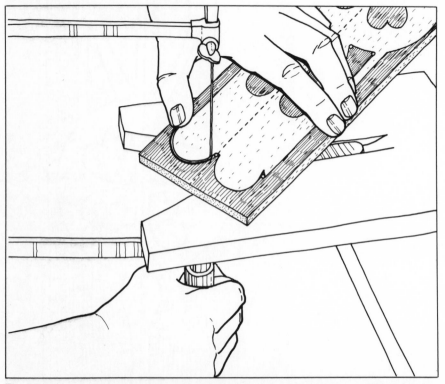

Fig. 20-5. Use a fretsaw and V board to clear away the waste. Make sure that you hold the saw so that the blade is at 90 degrees to the working face of the wood.

Work along the pencil lines, trying all the while to keep the saw blade at 90 degrees to the working face of the wood. When you come to working one of the "windows," remove the blade from its frame, pass it through one or the other of the pilot holes, refit it in its frame, and then continue sawing as already described. Keep the blade moving at a steady pace, and when you come to an angle or curve, try to keep both the wood and saw moving so that the blade is presented with the line of next cut. Continue until you have fretted out the flat ¼-inch-thick blank. NOTE: if you are a beginner, then you are going to break blades. Make sure that you have a couple of spare packs.

Rounding Off

When you have fretted out the profile and all the "windows" and you feel that the overall balance between wood and space is as it should be, then clear away the bench clutter and set out your graded sandpaper and the knife.

Take the knife and, with a delicate paring action, go over the whole project, trimming off all unpleasant corners and rough edges (FIG. 20-6). As you get closer to the envisaged form, work with greater care. Continue slowly and only remove the finest wisps of wood.

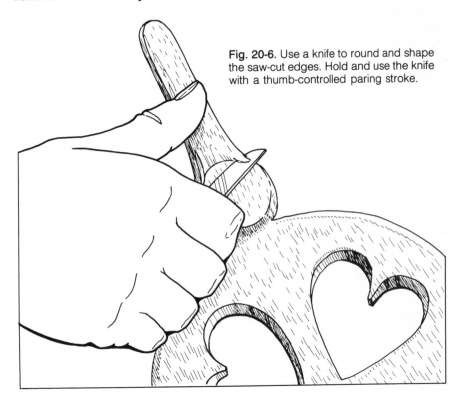

Fig. 20-6. Use a knife to round and shape the saw-cut edges. Hold and use the knife with a thumb-controlled paring stroke.

Proceed, running the knife around the two disks at the top of the form, edging the various heart-shaped windows, sharpening up the tight angles, and so on. Be extra cautious when you are working the fragile short-grain areas at the center of the four hearts. Take care that you never let the blade run into the grain of the wood, and always work with a totally controlled double-handed action.

When you have achieved a well-considered, crisp form, take up a piece of fine sandpaper and rub down all the edges and angles until they run together. Don't overwork the sanding stage, and certainly don't try to remove all the tool marks. Just settle for bringing the form together.

Chip Carving

When the whole form has been trimmed and rubbed down, put it to one side. Refresh your eye by having another look at the working drawings and the inspirational designs. See how the carved design is really made up from a framework of incised lines, bands of little three-cut triangular nicks that run around the profile, and a dozen or so larger and deeper chip-carved pockets.

When you have some understanding of how the design has been put together and you have perhaps had a trial run on a scrap of wood, then take a compass, or better still a pair of dividers. Go over the project, stepping off, setting out, and generally scribing all the arcs and circles that go to make up the design (FIG. 20-7). Don't worry too much if your circles aren't quite central or if the bands and borders are a bit askew. Just settle for a guide grid that is adjusted to follow the wood.

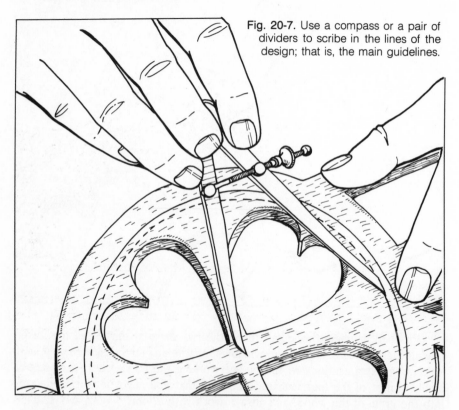

Fig. 20-7. Use a compass or a pair of dividers to scribe in the lines of the design; that is, the main guidelines.

Take a soft pencil and go over the wood, marking in the approximate position of the different chip cuts. Now take your fine-pointed knife and set-in the main lines of the grid with delicate incised cuts. That is to say, make two side-by-side cut lines—one at an angle to the other—so that a thin sliver of wood curls away.

When you have cut-in the grid in this manner, then start to work the various ribbons of chip carving. For each of the little chip cuts, make two stop cuts down into the wood. These should meet each other at about a 90-degree angle. Then slide the point of the knife in at an angle toward the stop cuts and lift out the little triangle of wood (FIG. 20-8). The secret of success is a well set out grid and a sharp blade.

Fig. 20-8. When you come to working the chip-carved design, cut in with a sharp-pointed knife and then remove the waste with slicing angled cuts.

When you come to working the larger and deeper triangular pockets, meaning the triangles at the intersections, take the knife and cut straight down into the wood so that there are three linked cuts that run from center to corner. When this has been done, approach in turn each of the three smaller triangles as already described. That is to say, hold the knife blade at a sloping angle, then slide it in toward the stop cuts, and lift out the triangular wedge of wood. Do this with each of the three facets that go to make up a large triangular pocket, and then go on to the next cut.

FINISHING

When you have cut-in all the lines and nicks that go to make up the design, and when you have also considered cutting dates and initials, then stand back from your work and be supercritical. Ask yourself: Could the designs be deeper?

Is there room for perhaps another band of pattern? Could the delicate bridges of wood be even finer? Spend time bringing the project to order.

This done, take a scrap of the finest sandpaper and swiftly wipe the wood over to remove all burrs and rough areas. Finally rub the project over with a little beeswax polish, use a soft brush to burnish the wood to a dull sheen, and the job is done.

- When you are clearing away the "windows" of waste, be careful that you don't twist the saw blade and so split the fragile short-grain bridges of wood.

- Chip-carving knives need to be razor sharp. At the start of the project spend time with the oilstone bringing the tools to a keen edge.

- When you are using the dividers, be careful that the points don't run into the grain and split the wood.

PROJECT 21

MAKING A *Bowl* IN THE
English Pole Lathe
Greenwood Tradition

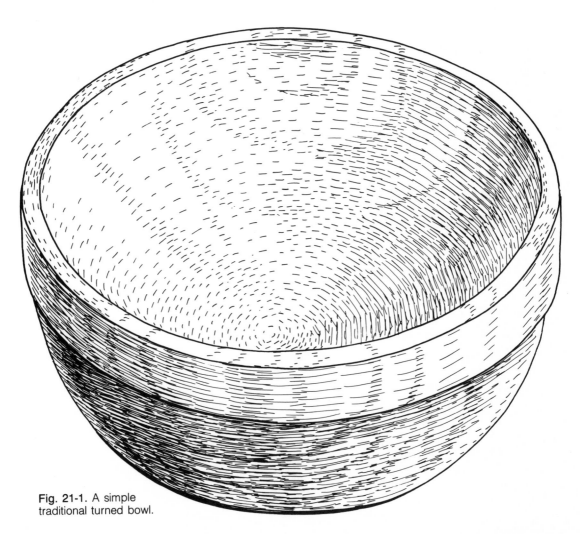

Fig. 21-1. A simple traditional turned bowl.

Wood-turning lathes have been around for at least 3,000 years. An Egyptian tomb painting shows a primitive, two-person lathe with the turner managing the wood and the gouge, while a helper operates a wheel-driven belt drive.

As to when the lathe first appeared in England, all that is known is that there are examples of turned bowls and turned wheel hubs that are at least 2,000 years old. By the Middle Ages, the lathe was well established, but of course it was not the continuous-drive type as we now understand it, but a backwards-and-forwards reciprocal-movement, pole-driven lathe, (see page 9). In 1909, William Lawrence, a writer for *The Country Home*, describes a bowl-maker's pole lathe as follows. "There are two massive upright posts set in the ground so that they are about 4-6 ft. apart. Linking these two posts and bridging the gap there is a huge flat beam or 'bed.' Mortised and wedged into the bed and set about 2-3 ft. apart there are two short upright head-and-tail stocks or 'poppet posts.' Coming out of these posts, pointing towards each other and parallel with the bed there are two spiked iron mandrels or pivots. The treadle is connected to the top of a sprung pole by a strong leathern strap, and this on its way passes round one or other of the mandrills and on down towards the treadle."

The method of making a greenwood bowl on such a lathe is beautifully simple. A block of green, or *wet*, wood—it is best to use elm, chestnut, or sycamore—is in turn cut into a lump, worked with an axe until it is roughly bowl shaped, and pivoted between the two spikes. When the treadle is pressed down, the wood spins toward the turner; when it is released, the wood spins back in the opposite direction. The turner thrusts his gouge forward and in on the downward stroke, and rests or withdraws it on the upward stroke. When the turner has worked the outside of the bowl, he then uses a long, hooked knife to work the inside. Up until World War I, bowl turners were able to turn whole nests of bowls from single baulks of greenwood using this method. Such bowls, varying in diameter from 3 to 24 inches, and selling for as little as fourpence, were used for general household and dairy work (FIG. 21-1).

Materials

A greenwood log about 8 inches in diameter and 4 inches deep
PVA glue

Tools

A wood-turning lathe, set at a low speed
A selection of wood-turning gouges and scrapers
A sharp axe, a chopping block
Calipers
Cardboard for templates
Scissors
Tracing paper, a pencil, a ruler
A hand drill and bit
A scrap of 1-inch-thick plywood
A workbench

Fig. 21-2. Inspirational designs

A modern
Norwegian
painted bowl

A cut,
decorated
Swedish bowl

A nineteenth century
painted Norwegian bowl

A nest of bowls
turned from a single
block of wood, English

An English bowl with a
subtle decorative rim

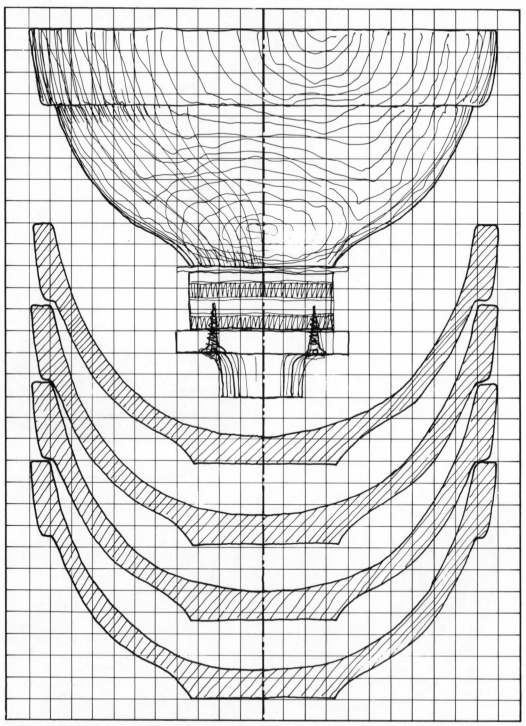

Fig. 21-3. Working drawings—the grid scale is about 4 squares to 1 inch. Note how the bowl is fixed to the faceplate via a wood and paper chuck, and see also how the bowls nest in each other.

DESIGN AND TECHNIQUE

Before you start this project, visit a rural or folk museum and view examples of ordinary wood-turned household and dairy bowls that were made before c. 1920. See how these bowls always have about them a special, "made for the hands" quality; that is to say, they are thick-walled, smooth-curved, uncomplicated forms that were made to serve a particular need. For example, there are soup bowls that are just the right size to be cupped in two hands; there are bowls that are designed to be used in the making of butter; there are bowls made for chopping herbs.

Bowls of this type and character tend to be beautifully unpretentious and nearly always without decoration (FIG. 21-2). Some folk societies did paint and stain their special turned wares. For example, in Sweden they decorated commemorative bowls with rosemaling or rose designs, and many European American turners stained their bowls and then whittled simple designs through the stain to reveal the white wood beneath. In England, however, traditional turners have always favored plain wares: a subtle turned border-rim maybe, or a smooth-curved foot ring, but no color or brushwork.

When you have looked at and handled as many turned bowls as possible, then go back to your workshop and draw out a number of bowl profiles (FIG. 21-3). Don't try for anything overfancy; just draw out bowls that are about 6 inches in diameter and about 3 to 4 inches deep.

When you have achieved a good profile, trace off the inside and outside forms. Pencil-press transfer the traced lines through to the template card.

Preparing the Wood and First Cuts

Take your lump of greenwood, and make sure that it is free from heart splits and dead, soft areas. Now set it out on a chopping block and with an axe, adze, large gouge, or another tool of your choice, knock off all the corners and rough stuff until you have a rough dome-shaped lump.

This done use long screws to secure the broad sawn face of the wood to a faceplate (FIG. 21-4). Now mount the faceplate on the lathe, and check the machine over, making sure that all is as it should be. Then set out your tools so that they are close at hand. Set the lathe at a slow speed, check that the wood isn't going to strike the bed of the lathe or the tool rest, make sure that your face is shielded, and then start to work.

First cut back all the high spots and gradually work in until you have roughed out the basic form. Checking with the template and the calipers, and using a gouge or another tool of your choice, establish the rim, the sweeping side curve, the little curve at the foot rim, and the flat bottom of the bowl (FIG. 21-5).

Working the Rough

Take the blank off the lathe and then, using a plywood disk, glue, and a sheet of newspaper, mount a glue-and-paper chuck on the flat-faced foot of the bowl.

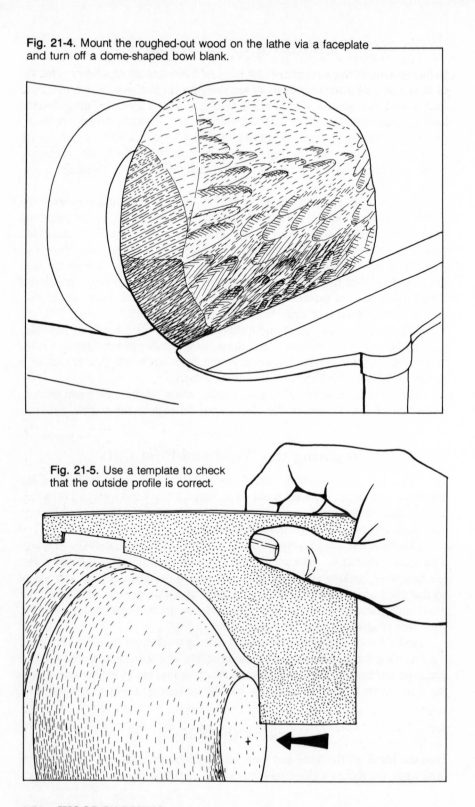

Fig. 21-4. Mount the roughed-out wood on the lathe via a faceplate and turn off a dome-shaped bowl blank.

Fig. 21-5. Use a template to check that the outside profile is correct.

When the glue is dry, give the wooden chuck a knock, just to make sure that it is a secure fixture, then screw it to a faceplate and remount the wood on the lathe. Now take the drill and the bit, and bore a pilot hole down through the depth of the bowl. Stop short about ¾ inch clear of the bowl's base. This done, use the gouge to clear away the face of the wood at what will be the bowl's rim (FIG. 21-6).

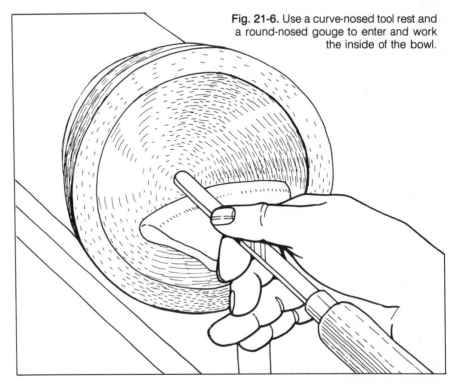

Fig. 21-6. Use a curve-nosed tool rest and a round-nosed gouge to enter and work the inside of the bowl.

Check with the calipers, then enter the wood, set out the thickness of the bowl walls, and start to clear away the waste (FIG. 21-7). Don't attempt to work a finished form; just go for a rough that has walls that are uniformly about ¾ to 1 inch thick. Finally, take the bowl off the lathe and put it in a cool, even atmosphere for about ten days or so until it has dried off.

Fine Turning

When the bowl has dried off—and this might well take longer than ten days, depending on the original wetness of the wood, the thickness of the bowl walls, and the conditions of the drying room—remount the bowl on the lathe. As likely as not, the bowl will have warped slightly and maybe even have developed some splits. They shouldn't be a problem, however, if the walls of the bowl are of a generous, even thickness.

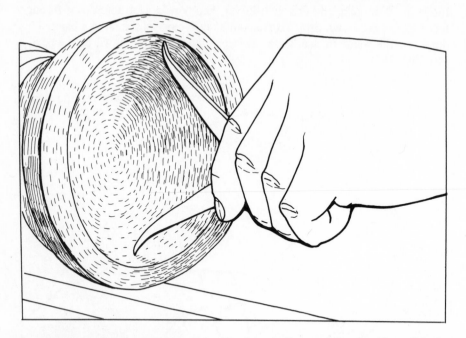

Starting with the outside of the bowl, and all the while checking with the template, cut back until the sizes are right. Finish off the outside of the bowl with sandpaper and beeswax.

You can now work the interior of the bowl in like manner. Then sandpaper and wax it.

FINISHING

When you reckon the bowl to be well turned, rubbed down, and waxed, take it from the lathe, support it rim-side down on the workbench, unscrew the faceplate, and then use a flat chisel and a mallet to cut back the wood-glue-and-paper chuck (FIG. 21-8).

This done, select a sharp, shallow-curved gouge and trim back the face of the foot until it is ever so slightly concave. Finally, give the bowl a generous waxing, leave it in a cool, dry atmosphere for a week or two, give it a good burnishing with a dry cloth, and the job is done.

Fig. 21-8. Unscrew and remove the metal faceplate, support the bowl rim side down on the workbench, and then use an old plane iron or some such to cut off the wooden chuck. Finally hollow the base slightly with a curved gouge.

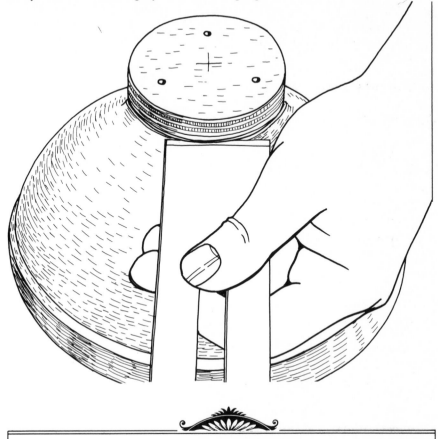

- The more time you spend at the roughing-out stage, the easier the initial turning will be.

- It is always a good idea to wear goggles and a mask when turning, but especially so at the roughing out stage when chips and splinters are flying.

- When you are screwing the faceplate to the glue-and-paper chuck, be careful that the screws aren't so long that they go right through the chuck and into the foot of the bowl.

- If, when you have worked the rough, it looks to be warping or splitting, quickly cover it in wax paste and extend the drying time.

MAKING A
Cradle
IN THE
American Pilgrim Tradition

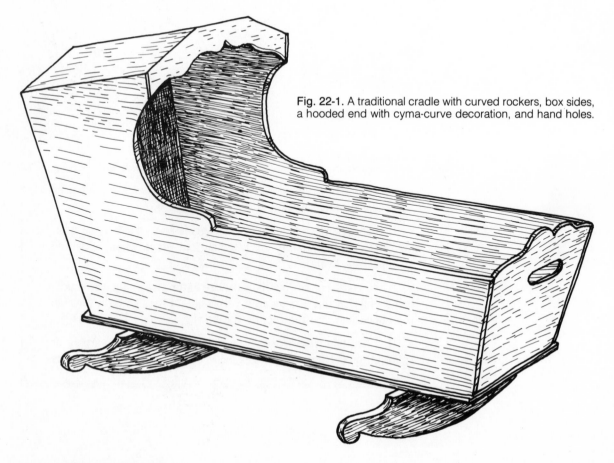

Fig. 22-1. A traditional cradle with curved rockers, box sides, a hooded end with cyma-curve decoration, and hand holes.

Fig. 22-2. Inspirational designs—three cradle types.

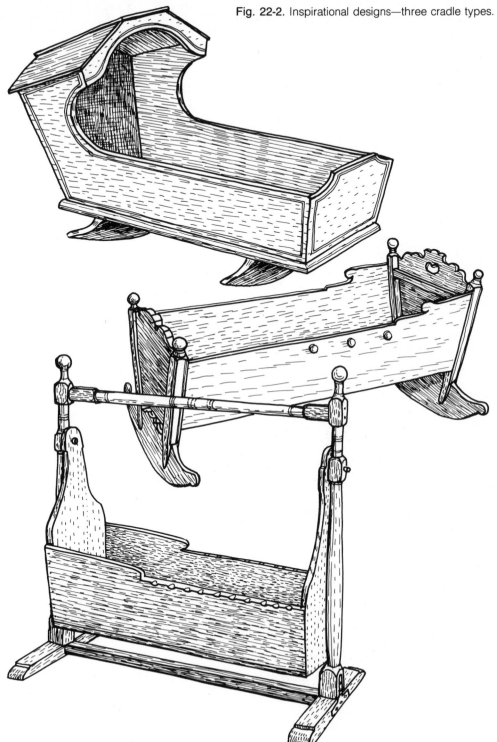

When the English Pilgrams and Puritans decided to "build a pure and godly New England" in America, they knew that times were going to be hard. In 1620 when the Mayflower set sail with 149 people on board, records indicate that her hold was crowded, there were very few personal possessions, and strangely enough, hardly any woodworking tools. So what did the settlers and pioneers do shelter and furniture in the New World? Well in the first instance, they lived in holes in the ground and made do with stick-and-stone benches and tables. Later, of course, when times got better, then the sober and industrious New Englanders soon set-to and started to make simple, functional pieces of furniture like beds, boxes, benches, tables, cribs, and cradles.

As to design, although they couldn't help but make pieces that reminded them of back home, the pioneer way of life demanded that they adapt and modify designs, techniques, and materials to suit their new conditions. So it was that, when the pioneers made say a cradle, they still continued to work all manner of beautiful sweeping *cyma curves* (traditional concave and convex double curves) into the hoods, end board and rockers (FIG. 22-1). Nevertheless, they did simplify the techniques and go for easy-to-work woods like pine and maple, and for the most basic butt-edge slab-box contruction. So, whereas an English cradle of c. 1625 would have been paneled up in oak, secured with pegged stiles, have turned and molded posts, and be laboriously carved and painstakingly polished, the New England counterpart would have been split straight out of easy-to-work, wide-girth, greenwood, (usually pine) and then simply box-jointed and fixed with pegs, or if they were lucky, nails. American furniture of this early period is often referred to as *Pilgrim*, or *kitchen hearth*.

Materials

A quantity of top-quality, best-faced, ½-inch-thick multilayer plywood (see working drawings)
Two pieces of prepared pine at 5½x1½ inches and 56 inches long, for the rockers
A quantity of brass panel pins
PVA glue
Beeswax

Tools

A quantity of cardboard for templates
Tracing paper, scissors, masking tape
A bow saw
A large coping saw, a straight saw
A hand drill and a ¼-inch drill bit
A 1½-inch-diameter cylindrical saw blade or hole saw
A keyhole or pad saw
A pack of graded sandpapers, a hammer
A couple of Surform shapers

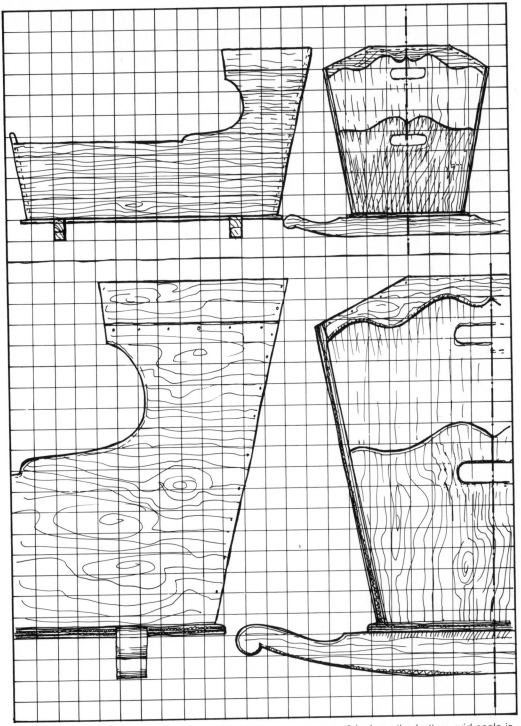

Fig. 22-3. Working drawings—the top grid scale is 1 square to 3 inches; the bottom grid scale is 2 squares to 3 inches.

DESIGN AND TECHNIQUE

Have a look at our various inspirational designs (FIG. 22-2) and working drawings (FIG. 22-3) and see how, to a greater or lesser extent, all the cradles relate to a simple five-board, box-built format. That is to say, the boards are lap-butted end to edge and then pin-fixed. See also how the project cradle has very simple and characteristic cyma curves worked into the end board, the hood front, and the side boards. Note also how the sides of the cradle spring up from a baseboard and gradually grow in width and breadth to make the characteristic narrow-based, wide-rimmed ark form.

When you have studied our drawings, take a trip to a folk museum and look at examples of country cribs and cradles made between 1620 and 1900. Sit down with a sketch pad, and make as many working and detail drawings as possible. Note different styles—the ornately pieced and carved cradles as made by the Pennsylvania Dutch, the lovely sweepy-curved Swedish cradles, the beautifully simple Shaker adult cradles, and so on.

See how although we have stayed with a traditional design, we have slightly updated the techniques and used best quality multi-ply, rather than thin-board, pine. NOTE: by *best quality multiply*, we mean a plywood that is made up in $\frac{1}{16}$-inch-thick veneers and has two good faces. WARNING: avoid coarse-centered "stout heart" or "Malaysian" plywood. Certainly materials of this character are about half the cost, but they are difficult to cut, impossible to finish, and crumbly edged.

Making the Templates and Building a Prototype

When you have decided just how you want your cradle to be, then make a scaled "front" and "side" working drawing, as illustrated in FIG. 22-3. Now, using the working drawings as a guide and being ready to adjust and modify the design to suit, use cardboard, scissors, pencil, ruler, and masking tape to build a full-size prototype (FIG. 22-4). By trial and error establish the exact size of the panels, the base, the two sides, the two ends, and the small hood pieces.

Spend time building the cardboard prototype, then stand back and be critical. Ask yourself: Could the sides come up at a greater angle? Does perhaps the hood make the cradle top heavy? Could the base be narrower or shorter? All these details need to be well considered before you cut the wood.

When you have achieved a good, full-size, perfectly fitting, working model, note the direction of the grain and carefully transfer the measurements to the working face of your sheet of plywood. Finally, when you are sure that your sizes and measurements are right, take a soft pencil and label all faces and edges.

Cutting and Working the Blanks

First use the straight saw to swiftly cut the wood into manageable pieces. Then secure the wood in the vise. With the coping and bow saw, carefully fret around the drawn shapes. Pay particular attention to the various decorative curves. Aim to work them so that they are smooth flowing and symmetrical.

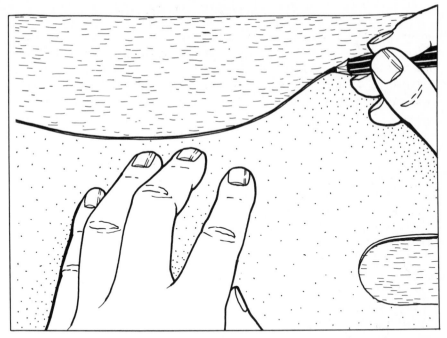

Fig. 22-4. Make full-size cardboard templates to work a well-fitting design. Use the templates to transfer the profiles through to the wood.

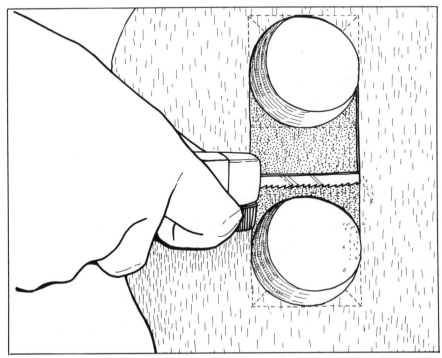

Fig. 22-5. Use a 1½-inch hole saw to cut and work the handle holes. Clear the between-hole waste with a keyhole saw.

As you are working, be mindful that the line of cut needs to be worked on the outside, or the waste side, of the drawn lines. Continue, maneuvering both the wood and one or other of the saws until you have cut out all the blanks.

Now, one piece at a time, set the end boards in the vise and establish the position of the hand hole (FIG. 22-5). When you have checked the size, position, and symmetry of the holes, take the 1½-inch hole saw and, being careful that you don't force or twist the tool and so splinter the wood, clear away the circular areas of waste at either end of the holes. Now use the keyhole/pad saw to clear away the waste between the holes.

This done, have a look at the blanks and the working drawings. Note which edges need to be square and which need to be rounded, and then work the wood with rasp and sandpaper accordingly.

Making the Rockers

Set the two lengths of pine out on the work surface, take a tracing of the rocker from the working drawing, and pencil-press transfer the traced lines through to the working faces of the wood. Carefully hatch in the waste areas.

It might help at this stage if you refresh your eye by looking at your collection of inspirational designs. See how the various rocker designs have the most beautiful, gentle, flowing curves and scroll ends.

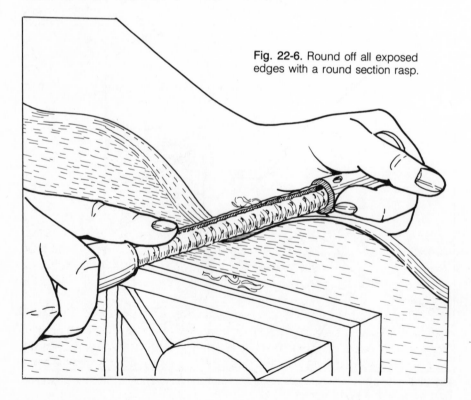

Fig. 22-6. Round off all exposed edges with a round section rasp.

When you are sure that all is correct, secure the wood in the vise and use the bow saw to clear away the waste. Now, take the tools of your choice—the round Surform, a drawknife, spokeshave, or whatever—and work the wood to a nicely curved, round-edged profile (FIG. 22-6). Watch out for the areas of relatively fragile short grain at the scroll ends. Finally, take the pack of graded sandpapers and rub the wood down to a good, smooth finish.

PUTTING TOGETHER AND FINISHING

When you have worked the eleven pieces that go to make up the project—the two rockers, the base, the four sides, the three hood pieces, and the decorative hood strip—set out the PVA glue, the hammer, and the pins, and start to put the cradle together (FIG. 22-7). As to the order of working, you might choose to work from the base up, or then again you might glue and pin the four sides and then fix them to the base. The order of working doesn't matter, as long as the various pieces come together to make a sound form.

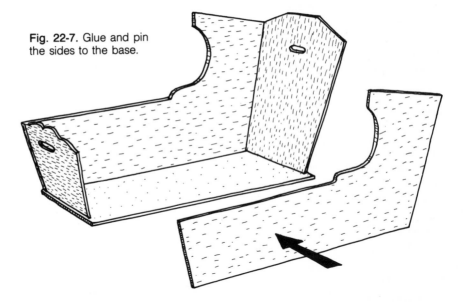

Fig. 22-7. Glue and pin the sides to the base.

It's very difficult to work with ten or so pieces of glue-covered wood that all want to move in a different direction. This being so, it is best if you build the cradle in stages, letting the glue dry before going on to the next stage. Be prepared to adjust and modify the pieces so that they come together to make a good fit.

When you come to fitting the rockers, set them out on a simple block-and-nail jig (FIG. 22-8), then you will be able to work without the whole project rocking backwards and forwards. Glue and pin the box to the rockers, then just to be on the safe side secure each rocker with a couple of brass countersunk screws.

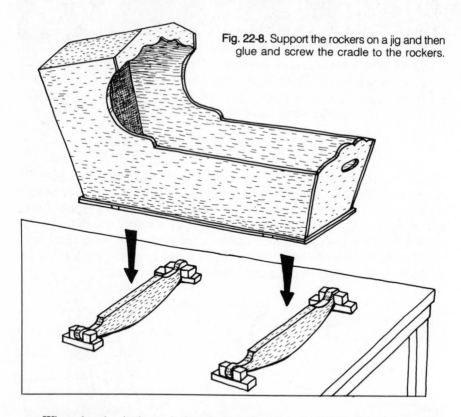

Fig. 22-8. Support the rockers on a jig and then glue and screw the cradle to the rockers.

When the glue is dry, rub the whole project down with the finest sandpapers and wipe the wood over with a damp cloth. When you consider the cradle well worked, up-end it and sign and date the base. Finally take a soft cloth and a generous amount of beeswax polish and burnish the wood to a creamy butter shine, and the job is done.

- If you choose to use thin pine boards, rather than sheets of plywood, you might need to slightly modify the design to take into account the position of the butt-glued board edges. If you do decide to use pine rather than ply, be extra careful when you are working the various decorative curves that you don't split the wood.

- You might consider painting or stenciling the finished cradle in one of the American decorative traditions. (See other projects.)

PROJECT 23

MAKING AND CARVING A
Plank-Back Spinning Stool
IN THE
Country-Cottage Tradition

Fig. 23-1. A traditional spinning stool with a carved plank back, a carved seat, and four simple, section wedge-fixed legs.

Peg legs, scabelle, spindle, stick, and slab backs are all chairs and stools that might be described as being rustic, peasant-made, or belonging to the archetypal country-cottage chair tradition. In New England, there are basic plank-back, stick-legged, wedge-tenoned chairs known as *peg legs*. In eighteenth and nineteenth century rural Italy, there were rather more ornate three-legged, scroll-back chairs known as *scabelle*. In Poland, there are heavy slab-seat, plank-back chairs called *mountain cottage chairs,* or *Podhale stools*. The Pennsylvania Dutch had a distinctive type of country chair that they called a *Moravian chair*. In England there were stools and chairs that were known as *Orkney spinning stools* (FIG. 23-1). I could go on and on.

Chairs and stools of this type and character don't really belong to any specific country, but rather are found wherever there is a peasant, folk-primitive, kitchen hearth furniture-making tradition. These chairs and stools are linked, not so much by period or design, but rather by the fact that they were all worked, built, and carved by rural, primitive, country craftsmen whose humble and honest aim was to do no more than build a functional seat.

Certainly these stools and chairs are sometimes pierced and carved, as in this project, but they are all characterized by their direct, primitive, uncluttered, plank construction. Not for these old country rustics, screws, nails, fancy paddings and such like; just a flat slab seat, a plank back tenoned and wedged directly into the seat, and three or four slightly splayed knife-worked legs.

Materials

A slab of rough-sawn 1½-inch-thick, half-seasoned oak about 36 inches long and about 24 inches wide.

Tools

A straight saw
A coping, bow, or frame saw
A mallet
A brace or hand drill
A spokeshave or a drawknife
A straight chisel
A straight gouge
A V-section tool
A spoon-bit gouge
Workshop items like a ruler, pencils, a compass, a square, a clamp, and rough work-out paper

---

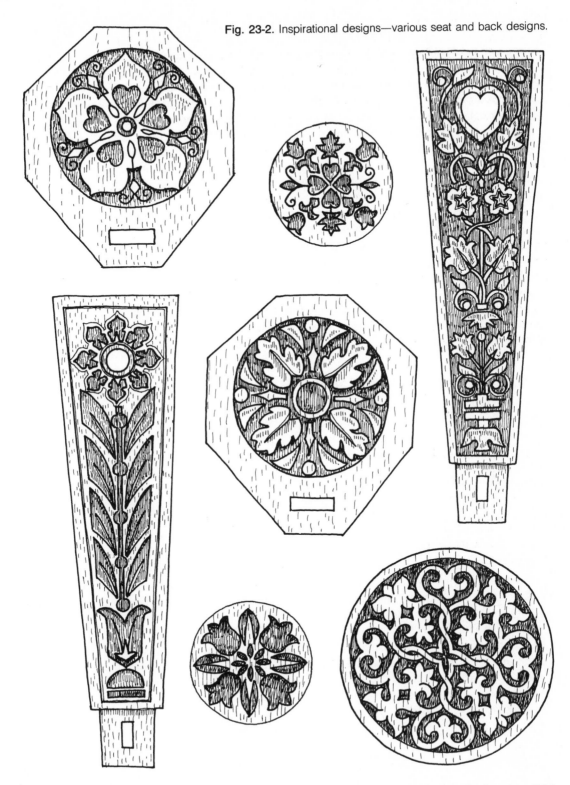

Fig. 23-2. Inspirational designs—various seat and back designs.

DESIGN AND TECHNIQUE

Before you put tool to wood, throw away all your preconceived ideas on how a chair ought to be made, and try to fit yourself into the shoes of a never-done-it-before pioneer settler or a peasant wood carver. You are using "in-the-rough" found wood; you only have a few basic tools; and you are seeking, to the best of your ability, to make a serviceable, simple, strong, slightly decorative chair.

Have a good look at the inspirational details (FIG. 23-2) and working drawings (FIG. 23-3), and see that our chair has a seat about 14x16 inches; a 30-inch-long, pierced, plank back that tapers from 8 inches wide at the top to about 4 inches wide at the tenon shoulders; and four slightly tapered octagonal-sectioned stick legs.

When you have studied all the working drawings and details, visit a museum and view as many folk-made chairs as possible. This done, take a large sheet of gridded work-out paper and draw up a full-size master design. Now pin all your inspirational drawings up around the working area, clear the workbench of all clutter, and set out all your tools and materials so that they are comfortably at hand.

Finally, set your wood out on the workbench and give it a good checking over. Make sure that it is reasonably straight grained and free from warps, splits, shakes, and dead knots.

Marking Out and Setting Out

When you have checked your wood over for problems, and when you have considered all the tool, material, and technique implications of the project, then take your compass, ruler, and pencil and start setting out the design as illustrated. Measure and mark out the eight-sided seat slab, the four legs, the plank back, and the wedge. When you are reasonably sure that all is correct and as described, then clearly label the blanks "seat," "legs," etc.

When you are happy with the marking out, take a fine-toothed straight saw and cut out the profiles. Now before you start setting out the areas to be carved, take the seat slab, secure it to the bench with the clamp, and then with the shallow gouge bring the rough-sawn surface to a slightly rippled finish. Don't rush this stage, but rather enjoy the even rhythm of the work. Try to let the tool create its own very beautiful and characteristic, soft, dappled and gently scalloped texture. Continue until you have tooled both slabs—meaning all faces of both the seat and the back.

Refresh your eye by having another look at the working drawings. See how the motif within the 11-inch-diameter seat roundel is quartered, and set back from the front of the seat by about 1½ inches. Note also how the plank-back design is set within a border and decoratively pierced. Finally, take a tracing of your master design, and pencil-press transfer the traced lines through to the working face of the wood.

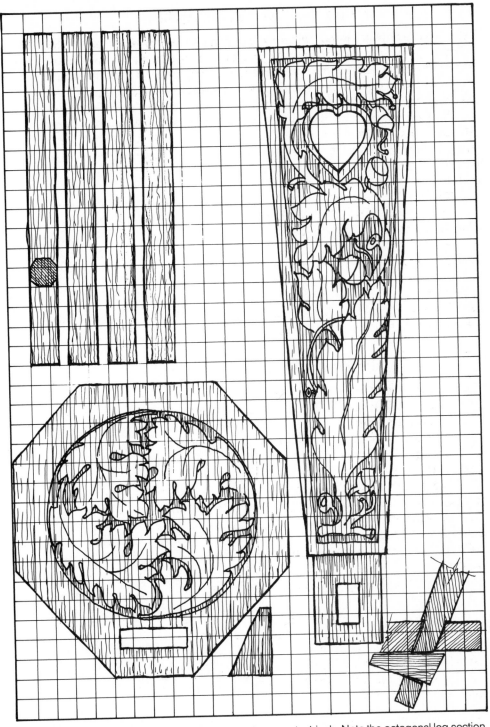

Fig. 23-3. Working drawings—the scale is about 1 square to 1 inch. Note the octagonal leg section, pieced heart in the back, and mortise-and-tenon wedge joint for back and seat.

Carving the Plank Back and Seat

After you have pencil-press transferred the lines of the design through to the working face of the wood, then you can start work on the plank back. Secure the wood in the vise, take the hand drill and the coping saw, and work the pierced heart motif (FIG. 23-4). Drill a starter hole, and then, with the coping saw blade held at 90 degrees to the working face of the wood, cut out the heart. Work with a steady even stroke, maneuvering and turning both the wood and the saw as you go.

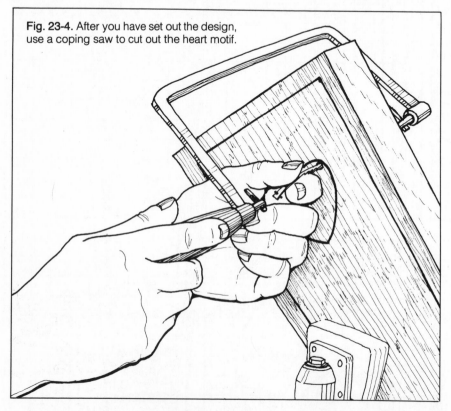

Fig. 23-4. After you have set out the design, use a coping saw to cut out the heart motif.

This done, clamp the wood flat and square on the bench, and set out your carving tools. Take the V-section tool and very carefully incise-outline the whole of the design. Work on the waste or ground side, and cut into the wood about ¼ inch outside the drawn lines.

As you run the tool around the design, you will be cutting both with and across the grain. Hold the tool with both hands, one hand guiding and the other pushing. Work with short, shallow, controlled strokes. As you are working, have your wits about you and be ready to stop short and pull back if you feel the tool running out of control or digging too deeply into the grain. At this stage, you shouldn't need to use the mallet; just put your shoulder behind the tool and try to cut a smooth, shallow V-section trench.

When you have incised the whole outline, then take the straight chisel and the gouge and set-in. That is to say, hold the tool in one hand so that the handle is leaning slightly over the design, and then cut into the lines of the motif with short, lively taps of the mallet. Try all the time, as you are working, to keep the depth of cut constant and at about ⅛ to ¼ inch deep. Aim to establish a clean, sharp-edged design.

Now take the spoon-bit gouge and cut a broad trench on the ground side of the V-section cut. Then, when you have established the depth of the lowered ground, chop out the waste (FIG. 23-5). Aim to leave the whole lowered ground area smooth and even, but not so overworked that you can't see the tool marks.

Fig. 23-5. After you have cut in the design with an incised line, clear away and lower the waste ground.

Finally, work around the now raised motifs and make sure that all the nooks and angles are free from bits and burrs. Don't undercut the edges. NOTE: some carvers lower the unwanted ground before they set-in. If you have doubts as to the order of work, have a trial run on a scrap of wood.

Take a look at the acorns-and-leaves design, as illustrated, and see how the forms have been worked in rather a straightforward and mechanical manner.

Now, take the straight gouge and work around the raised design, all the while cutting away and rounding the sharp edges. Don't try to work subtle curves or undercuts, but rather go for swift, direct stylization.

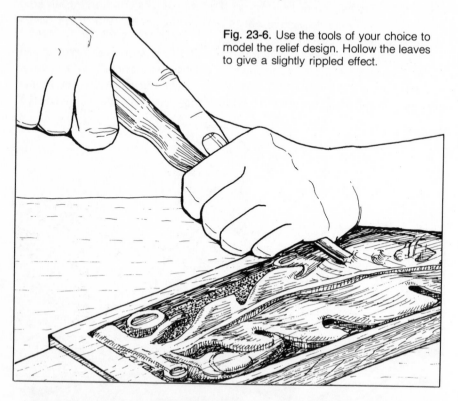

Fig. 23-6. Use the tools of your choice to model the relief design. Hollow the leaves to give a slightly rippled effect.

When you have rounded up the leaf forms, then work from side to center and scoop out the wood so as to leave them all slightly dished (FIG. 23-6). Take care, as you are dishing, that you don't damage short-grain areas or cut into the raised leaf veining.

Continue cutting and running the tools across the grain, and working around the forms until you feel that you have taken the carving as far as you want it to go (FIG. 23-7). Don't fuss and worry the design; just try to keep it simple, bold, and direct. When you have worked the plank back, carve the seat in like manner.

Working the Back-to-Seat Joint

Have a close look at the working drawings and see how the tapered back is tenoned and rabbeted so that it enters the seat mortise at an oblique angle of about 100 to 110 degrees. Now, using the tools of your choice, cut and work the plank tenon and the seat mortise to fit, then gently pare away at the shoulders of the tenon, until the back strikes the seat smoothly and cleanly.

This done, cut a mortise in the plank-back tenon. Make sure that it pierces the wood at an angle parallel to the seat, then cut and fit a wedge, as illustrated.

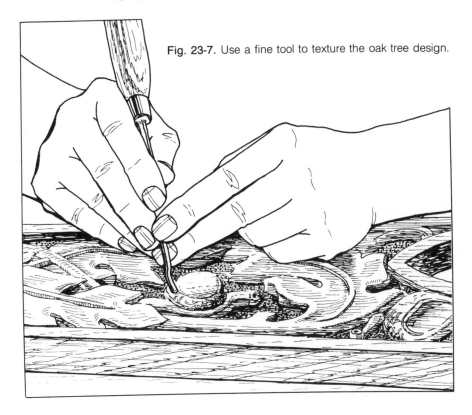

Fig. 23-7. Use a fine tool to texture the oak tree design.

Working the Legs and Getting It All Together

Take the leg blanks one stick at a time, secure them in the vise, and then shape them with the spokeshave or drawknife until they are gently tapered and octagonal in section (FIG. 23-8). Aim to take the taper from about 1½ inches at the bottom to about 1¼ inches at the top.

When you have cut and worked all four legs, place the seat slab face down on the workbench and bore four carefully considered and angled holes. Now taper the ends of the legs so that they are a good, stiff fit in the holes. Cut wedge slots, and glue, fit, and fix, as illustrated in FIG. 23-9.

When the legs have been wedge-tenoned into the seat, then insert the plank-back tenon into the seat mortise, and bang home the holding wedge. This done, adjust the chair so that it sits firm and four-square, and then go over the whole project with a small gouge, bringing it to good order.

Finally, when you have tidied up all the sharp edges and have left the surface looking dappled and tooled, dust the wood over with a stiff brush, lay on a couple of coats of beeswax, and the job is done.

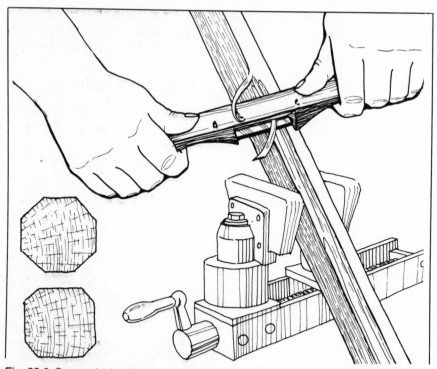

Fig. 23-8. Secure the leg blanks in the jaws of a vise and then take a drawknife or spoke-shave and cut away the corners of the wood to work the octagonal leg section.

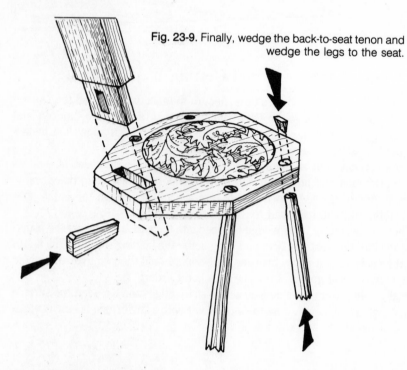

Fig. 23-9. Finally, wedge the back-to-seat tenon and wedge the legs to the seat.

- You might modify this project and say work a painted or chip-carved design. (See other projects.)

- When you come to fixing the leg wedge tenons, make sure that the little wedges are cut and fitted so that they run across the grain of the seat, as illustrated.

- If you think the slab seat looks a little on the heavy side, bevel the underedge with a gouge so that, edge on, the seat looks to be about ¾ inch thick.

- When you bore the leg holes, judge the angle by eye and watch out that you don't split or damage the wood. It is a good idea to drill from both sides.

Further Reading

THE ART OF THE PEOPLE IN AMERICA AND BRITAIN
Ayres, James
Published for exhibition in Manchester, England, 1985.

BRITISH FOLK ART
Ayres, James
Published by Barrie and Jenkins, London, 1977.

WILD FOWL DECOYS
Barber, Joel
Published by Dover, NY, 1954.

THE COMPLETE GUIDE TO DECORATIVE WOODWORK
Bridgewater, Alan and Gill
Published by Phaidon Oxford, 1986.

THE CRAFT OF WOODCARVING
Bridgewater, Alan and Gill
Published by David and Charles, 1981.

MAKING WOOD TOYS THAT MOVE
Bridgewater, Alan and Gill
Published by Sterling, 1987.

PRINTING WITH WOOD BLOCKS, STENCILS AND ENGRAVING
Bridgewater, Alan and Gill
Published by David and Charles, 1983.

STEP-BY-STEP WOODCARVING
Bridgewater, Alan and Gill
Published by Bell and Hyman, London, 1985.

A TREASURY OF WOODCARVED DESIGN
Bridgewater, Alan and Gill
Published by Van Nostrand, NY, 1981.

FOLK ART IN POLAND
Czarnecka, Irena
Published by Polonia Warsaw, 1957.

PEASANT ART IN SWEDEN, LAPLAND AND ICELAND
Holme, Charles
Published by The Studio, 1910.

TECHNIQUES IN AMERICAN FOLK ART
Lipman, Jean
Published by Dover, NY, 1972.

THE FLOWERING OF AMERICAN FOLK ART
Lipman, Jean
Published by Viking Press, NY, 1974.

ILLUSTRATED GUIDE TO SHAKER FURNITURE
Meader, Robert
Published by Dover, NY, 1972.

MAKING WHIRLIGIGS AND OTHER WIND TOYS
Pierce, Sharon
Published by Sterling, NY, 1985.

TREEN AND OTHER WOODEN BYGONES
Pinto, Edward
Published by Bell and Hyman, London, 1969.

ANTIQUE COUNTRY FURNITURE OF NORTH AMERICA
Shea, John
Published by Van Nostrand Reinhold, NY, 1975.

WHITTLING AND WOODCARVING
Tangerman, E.J.
Published by Dover, NY, 1962.

COMPLETE GUIDE TO WOODCARVING
Tangerman, E. J.
Published by Sterling, NY, 1984.

Index

A

acrylic paint, 1
adze, 1
apple wood, 1
ash, 1
axe, 1, 16

B

beech, 1
beeswax, 1
bending, 153, 154
bent gouges, 1
biscuit molds, 77
  design and technique for, 80
  finishing for, 84
  gouge and knife work, 80
  history of, 77
  setting out wood and first cuts, 80
  traditional design of, 79
  using plasticine to test design of, 82
  working drawing and grid scale for,
    81
black-line striping, 103
blanks, 30
blemish, 2
blocking in color, 103
bow saw, 2, 23
bowls, 219
boxwood, 2
brace and bit, 16, 164
bridge, 2
brushes, 2

burning, 202
burnishing, 3
butter molds, 128
butter roller, 127

C

C-clamp, 16
calipers, 3
carved chest, 96
  history of, 98
  inspirational designs for, 97
carved panels, 96
  black-line striping and blocking in
    colors, 103
  color grid for, 101
  design and technique for, 99
  history of, 98
  inspirational designs for, 97
  preparing ground and transferring
    design for, 99
  working drawing grid scale, 100
carver's chops, 14
chain cutting, 43
chair, Hitchcock, 177
check, 3
cherry, 3
chestnut, 3
chip knives, 17
chip-carving, 3, 117, 212
  design and technique for, 121
  distaff, 216
  finishing, 126

history of, 118
indicating depth of cuts in, 122
knife for, 4
setting in first cuts, 123
setting out roundel for, 121
traditional designs for, 119
working drawing grid scale for, 120
working triangular chip cuts in, 123
working zigzag border in, 125
chisel, 4, 16
cigar store Indian, 86
design and technique for, 90
details and patterns, 93
modeling the forms, 93
painting, 94
setting in and wasting, 90
setting out design and first cuts, 90
working drawing and grid scale for, 89
clamping, 4, 109
close-grained wood, 4
color grid, 101, 111, 192
combing paint, 102
comfort boards, 137
applying light colors, 145
applying shadow and tone in, 144
design and technique for, 139
fretting out figure and preparation, 142
highlights, varnishing, and finishing of, 145
history of, 138
inspirational designs for, 140
scale drawing for, 141
transferring design and blocking in, 143
compass, 4, 16, 120, 122, 216
coniferous trees, 13
cookie molds, 77
coping saw, 4, 16, 42, 164, 242
cradle, 228
assembly and finishing for, 235
cutting and working blanks for, 232
design and technique for, 232
history of, 230
making rockers for, 234
scale drawing for, 231
templates and prototype for, 232
traditional designs for, 229

cupboards, 158
cyma curves, 230

D
decay, 5
decoys, 106
color grid for, 111
design and technique for, 109
first cuts, gluing, clamping, 109
head carving for, 112, 113
history of, 108
painting and finishing, 114
priming for, 115
removing waste areas and working body, 112
setting out wood for, 109
traditional designs for, 107
working drawing grid scale for, 110
design, 5, 6
distaff, 208
chip-carving in, 212, 216
design and technique for, 212
finishing of, 217
fretting out design of, 214
history of, 210
inspirational designs for, 209
rounding off, 215
scale drawing for, 211
setting out design for, 212
transferring design of, 213
dividers, 16, 122, 216
dower chests, 98
drawing boards, 6
drawknife, 5, 16, 246
drill, 5
dummy boards, 138

E
Eaton, W.P., 178
elevations, 5
epigrams, 200

F
faces, 63
figure boards, 137
figureheads, 88
figures, 86
filler, 7
fine turning, 225

fingers, 149
finish, 7
first cuts, 7, 22, 60
flat-relief, 48
folk American fractur, 188
  inspirational designs for, 189
found wood, 7
fractur salt box, 187
fretsaw, 7, 214
fretting out, 23, 142, 214
further reading, 249

G

German springerle boards, 77
gluing, 7, 109
gouge, 7, 17, 33, 80
  V-section, 14
greenwood, 7, 220
grid, 7
ground, texturing, 55
grounding, 7

H

hammer, 17
hardwood, 7
hex motifs, 98
highlights, 25, 145
Hitchcock chair, 177
  design and technique for, 180
  dusting bronze powder on, 184
  history of, 178
  inspirational design for, 179
  laying ground, 182
  making stencil plates for, 182
  stencil scale drawings for, 181
  striping and finishing, 185
Hitchcock, Lambert, 178
hole saw, 233
holly, 7
hope chest, 98

I

incised carving, 8
inspirational material, 8

J

Jacobean carving, 48
Johnson, Jared, 178
joint, mortise and tenon, 244

K

keyhole saw, 8, 233
kitchen hearth furniture, 230
knife, 8, 80
knots, 9

L

lappers, 149
lathe, 9, 130, 133, 220
  history of, 220
  parts of, 220
Lawrence, William, 220
letter cutting, 34
lettering, 205
lime, 10
low-relief, 48
lowering ground, 10, 32, 54

M

mahogany, 10
mallet, 10
maquette, 10, 171
marking out, 10
milk paint, 148
modeling, 93
molds, 128
Moravian chair, 238
mortise and tenon joint, 244
mountain cottage chair, 238
Mr. Punch, 167
  design and technique for, 168
  history of, 168
  inspirational design for, 169
  making maquette for, 171
  modeling and detailing, 174
  painting, 174
  scale drawings for, 170
  setting out design and first cuts in, 171
  stuffed body for, 175
  whittling form of, 171

O

oak, 10
off-cuts, 10
Orkney spinning chair, 238

P

pad saw, 8

paint, 10
  aging or antiqueing, 25
  applying light colors in, 145
  applying shadow and tone, 144
  milk paint in, 148
parting cut, 42
pastry rollers, 127
  assembly of, 136
  carving wheel patterns and designs in, 135
  cross sectional view of, 132
  cutting pronged stirrup and pivot holes, 134
  design and technique for, 130
  main grid scale drawing for, 131
  parting off, 133
  traditional design for, 129
  turning main form for, 130
patterns, 93, 102
paw print, 102
pear, 10
peg legs, 238
pencil, 10
pencil-press transferring, 11, 22, 91
Pensylvania Dutch design, 188
piercing, 11, 43, 44, 233, 242
Pilgrim furniture, 230
pilot holes, 44
pine, 12
plank-back spinning stool, 237
Plasticine, 171
plum, 12
plywood, 232
Podhale stools, 238
poesies, 200
pole lathe, 9
polyvinyl acetate (PVA) glue, 12
preparing wood, 50
presses, 128
priming, 115
profiles, 12
prototype, 12
pulling together, 11
Punchinello, 167
puppets, 167
  inspirational designs for, 169

Q
quick finish, 12

R
racks, 157
rasps, 17
relief carving, 12
riffler, 12, 17
rippled grain, 102
rivet clinching, 153
rooster weather vane, 18
roughing out, 12
roughs, 223
round-up, 54
roundels, 121, 198
  blocking in color in, 204
  design and technique for, 202
  gold paint highlights and finish for, 206
  history of, 200
  inspirational designs for, 199
  lettering in, 205
  scale drawing for, 201
  setting out design for, 202
  tracing and transferring design of, 203
  wood burning in, 203
rubbing down, 12

S
salt box, 187
  assembly of, 193
  blocking in color and finishing, 196
  design and technique for, 190
  painting grid for, 192
  preparing ground and lining in, 195
  scale drawings for, 191
  setting out and first cuts in, 190
  shaping, 193
sapwood, 12
scabelle, 238
scoop gouge, 24, 54, 83
screwdrivers, 17
seasoned wood, 12
set square, 6
setting in, 12, 52, 90
setting out, 13, 22
shake, 13
Shaker carrier, 147
  cutting blanks for, 152
  design and technique for, 149
  handle and base for, 155

making and using templates for, 149
milk paint for, 148
scale drawing for, 151
steaming, bending, rivet-clenching in, 153
tapering and decorating lappers in, 152
traditional designs for, 150
Shakers, history of, 148
shelves, 158
ship's figureheads, 88
short grain, 13
signboards, 27
  design and technique for, 30
  inspirational designs for, 29
  letter cutting in, 34
sketchbook, 13
slipstone, 13, 17
smoking paint, 102
softwood, 13
spinning stool, 237
  assembly of, 245
  carving plank back and seat for, 242
  design and technique for, 240
  history of, 238
  inspirational designs for, 239
  marking out and setting out, 240
  scale drawings for, 241
  working back-to-seat joint in, 244
  working legs for, 246
spokeshave, 246
spoons, 38
stamps, 128
steam bending, 153
stencil, 11
stencil card, 13
stencil plates, 73, 180
stenciled chair, 177
stenciling, 13, 67, 180, 183
  bronze powder dust for, 184
  cutting of, 75
  cutting stencil plates for, 73
  design and technique for, 70
  detail of, 72
  history of, 68
  painting technique for, 76
  preparing ground, scoring grid, and painting, 70
  printing of, 74

scale drawings for, 181
traditional designs for, 69
stippling, 76
stop cuts, 13, 24, 35, 62
strapwork, 48
Surform, 13
sycamore, 13

T
T square, 6
templates, 149
  cradle, 232
  stencil, 73, 180
  wall shelf, 160
  wooden bowl, 224
tenon saw, 17
texturing effects, 55, 102, 244
tooled finish, 13
tracing paper, 13
treen, 127
trenching, 13
tulip motif, 47
  design and technique for, 50
  traditional designs for, 49
turning, 130

U
U-section gouge, 55
unseasoned wood, 7, 220

V
V-section tool, 14, 52
valet boards, 138
varnish, 145, 186
vise, 14, 17

W
wall hanging, 38
wall shelf, 157, 158
  assembly, finishing, painting, 165
  cutting wood to size and setting out for, 162
  design and technique for, 160
  drilling spoon holes for, 164
  inspirational designs for, 159
  making shelf lengths for, 163
  scale drawing for, 161
  template for, 160
  working end boards for, 162

waste ground, 14
  lowering of, 33, 54
wasting, 7, 90
weather vane sculpture, 18
  design and technique for, 20
  traditional designs for, 19
  whirligigs as, 58
Welsh love spoons, 38
  design and technique, 40
  traditional designs for, 39
wet wood, 7, 220
whirligigs, 57
  assembly of, 65
  design and technique, 60
  paddle arms for, 63
  painting, 64
  traditional designs for, 59
  whittling face for, 63
whittling, 14
  face, 63
  Mr. Punch, 171
windmills, 58
wood burning, 202
  setting design in, 204
wood preparation, 50

wooden bowl, 219
  design and technique for, 223
  fine turning in, 225
  finishing in, 226
  preparing wood and first cuts for, 223
  scale drawing for, 222
  traditional design for, 221
  using template to check profile of, 224
  working the rough in, 223
woodturning, 220, 225
woodworking tools, 14
workbench, 15
working drawings, 15
working face, 15
workouts, 15
workshop data, 1
worn highlights, 25

Y
yew, 15

Z
zigzag border, 125